EXPL⬤RE!

A
BOOK
of SCIENCE

Explorations in Science

PROGRAM AUTHORS

STEPHEN CAMPBELL

DIANA KAYE GOOLEY

LALIE HARCOURT

DOUG HERRIDGE

GILLIAN KYDD

SHERRY MAITSON

NANCY MOORE

BEVERLEY WILLIAMS

RICKI WORTZMAN

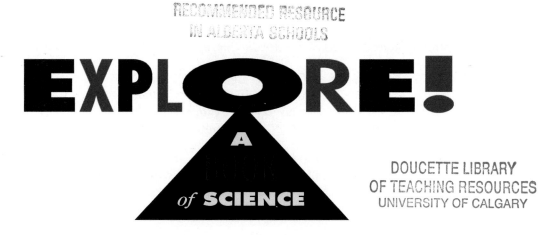

EXPLORE!
A BOOK of SCIENCE

JAY INGRAM

DOUG HERRIDGE
NANCY MOORE

Addison-Wesley Publishers Limited

Don Mills, Ontario • Reading, Massachusetts • Menlo Park, California
New York • Wokingham, England • Amsterdam • Bonn
Sydney • Singapore • Tokyo • Madrid • San Juan

Editorial Development *Susan Petersiel Berg • Mei-lin Cheung • Maggie Goh • Keltie Thomas • Theresa Thomas*

Design and Art Direction *Wycliffe Smith Design*
Electronic Production *Tony Delitala*
Cover Design *Wycliffe Smith • Tony Delitala*
Cover Photograph *Miller Comstock/H. Armstrong Roberts*

Acknowledgments for the selections appear on page 230.
See page 234 for a complete list of illustrators. See page 235 for a complete list of photographers.
The authors and publisher wish to thank Ms. Carol Huycke and the Grade Four classes at Oak Ridges Public School
for reviewing the manuscript and the design, and for their input, ideas, and help in the development of this book.

Scientific Reviewers
Dr. Shannon Berch, Department of Soil Science, University of British Columbia
Linda Ervine, Metro Toronto Zoo
Dr. Karen Goodrowe, Metro Toronto Zoo
Dr. Wayne Hawthorn, Department of Biology, University of Waterloo
Dr. Linda Heier, Assistant Professor of Radiology, Cornell University
Dr. Kenneth Pinder, Department of Chemical Engineering, University of British Columbia
Dr. Margaret E. Silliker, Department of Biology, De Paul University
Dr. Mason R. Yearian, Department of Physics, Stanford University

We are grateful to the following consultants:
Charles Barman, Ed.D., Associate Professor of Science Education, Indiana University
David Brummett, Ph.D., Math and Science Education Consultant, Palo Alto, California
Michael A. DiSpezio, M.A., Science Education Consultant, Cataumet, Massachusetts
Vallie Guthrie, Ph.D., Director, Greensboro Area Math and Science Education Center, North

Canadian Cataloguing in Publication Data

Ingram, Jay
Explore! : A book of science, 4

Includes index
ISBN 0-201-55509-3

1. Science — Juvenile literature. I. Herridge , Doug , 1954 —
II . Moore , Nancy , 1952 —
III . Title .

Q163.154 1992   j500   C92-093417-X

This book contains recycled product and is acid free. Printed and bound in Canada.

ISBN 0-201-55509-3

B C D E F — FR — 97 96 95 94

CONTENTS

GROWING wild

WHAT'S AHEAD

PLANT TALK

BY JAY INGRAM

You could live in a house full of plants, walk along a street lined with trees, or camp in a forest — and never realize that plants can talk to each other. But it's true. They do!

Of course, plants don't make any noises. And they don't wave their leaves at each other in a green version of sign language. So how do plants talk?

Smell

How do you know when somebody wearing perfume has walked by, or that something's rotten in the fridge? You smell. Plants can do that, too. Or at least the plant version of smell. Even though they don't have noses, they do have ways of detecting chemicals — and that's what smelling really is.

Say it with chemicals

Now you might think this is ridiculous — plants don't have any brains, so how could they think of something to say? Well, you're right. Nobody's saying they're smart. But they can still sense what's around them and respond with chemical messages.

Most "plant talk" is really plant warnings. There are two kinds: a plant that's being eaten will warn its neighbors that they're likely to be the next meal, and plants that are competing for the same territory will tell other plants to find their own piece of ground.

Where the antelope roam

In southern Africa, antelopes eat the leaves of a plant called acacia (a-KAY-sha). Normally, an acacia tree can survive providing a few leaves for an antelope snack. However, if there's a drought, or there are too many antelopes, then the trees are in trouble. A tree that's losing too many leaves to hungry antelopes releases a chemical called ethylene into the wind — 20 times more than an undamaged tree does. Any acacias that are downwind — even half a football field away — get a whiff of that ethylene. And they not only get the message clearly, but they know exactly how to respond.

An antelope nibbling on an acacia tree

3

An acacia that smells ethylene in the wind starts to make a chemical called tannin in its leaves. Tannin tastes terrible, and antelopes will usually avoid leaves that contain it. In fact, if antelopes eat too many tannin-filled leaves, they may even die. So the acacia that's being overeaten produces ethylene which tells it to make tannin. Nearby acacias can be alerted by the ethylene from other trees. Some scientists have suggested that sugar maples in North America do the same thing if they're being attacked by caterpillars.

Rooting for selfishness

But plants don't always help each other out. There may be a different kind of communication going on underground. Scientists have discovered that a common desert shrub, the creosote (KREE-uh-soat) bush, tells other desert plants to "get lost!" When the roots of a neighboring plant wander too close to the roots of the creosote, they receive an unfriendly message. Like the acacia tree, the creosote plant sends chemical messages that slow down — and even stop — other plant roots from growing. So the creosote doesn't have to worry about plant strangers taking over its territory — it won't let them get close enough.

Don't worry or get too excited. As far as we know, the carrots you chop for salad aren't sending any "don't grow" messages to your neighbor's garden.

Row of creosote bushes in the desert

A LITTLE MOZART, PLEASE

Experiments with several kinds of plants seem to prove that plants can sense different types of music. They even show strong likes and dislikes.

Corn, petunias, zinnia, and marigolds were used in one experiment with classical and rock music. Rock music caused some of the plants to grow much too tall and weak. They leaned away from the sound, as if trying to escape. The leaves of these plants were small and undeveloped. During the first week, the plants used large amounts of water, but their roots grew only about two centimetres after 18 days. All the marigolds were dead by the end of the second week.

Plants exposed to the classical music of Beethoven and Mozart grew toward the sound. They had healthy growth, with normal stems and leaves. They used less water than the plants exposed to rock music, and the root growth was heavy, up to 10 cm. The same thing happened when classical Indian music was played on the sitar, a stringed instrument. The plants grew more than 60 degrees toward the sound, which means that they were leaning about as far as they could without falling over!

Does this prove that plants can recognize different forms of music? Perhaps, but not as music. Since plants do not have hearing organs, the differences in wave patterns can only be felt as vibrations, but not heard, by the plants.

Maybe this means that plants think Beethoven has good vibes.

— Philip Barnard

Scientists are always repeating experiments to see if they come up with the same results. With a friend, try the musical experiment described. What kinds of music will you compare?

These tough plants
live through heat, pollution,
and lack of water.
They are ...

SIDEWALK SURVIVORS

BY VICKY McMILLAN

Some plants can grow in amazing places — where the soil is poor, where people walk on them all the time, and where there's hardly any place to put their roots. Most of us pass these plants every day. We call them weeds, and they grow right under our feet on the sidewalk!

Dirt is slowly filling in the spaces in this sidewalk grate, allowing small plants to take root.

This weed is a close relative of the lettuce that grows in our gardens. Its bright flowers give a splash of color to a drab city corner.

Try

How many unusual places can you find plants growing? How many different kinds of "pioneer" plants can you find? With a friend, create a map showing where hardy plants can be found and how they look.

Popcorn first appeared in Mexico over 80 000 years ago. The kernels were a little different from ours — harder and smaller. Scientists have found more popcorn than any other kind of corn around ancient Indian ruins.

7

Gardeners think of weeds as nuisances when they crowd out flowers and vegetables. Scientists think of them in a different way. Weeds are "pioneers." They are among the first plants to appear in hard-to-live-in places where more choosy plants can't grow. Sidewalk weeds sprout in tiny cracks in the pavement, growing in dirt blown in by the wind. Many live in

This plant is called pineapple weed because it smells like pineapple. Its leaves and stems are so tough and wiry that you can jump up and down on them without hurting the plant. Pineapple weed can grow where people frequently walk or along roadsides, where there is heavy traffic.

spots that are hot and dry, or where the soil and air are polluted by car exhaust or factory fumes.

Weeds brighten up our sidewalks and streets — and they show us that some plants have special ways of surviving even in the most difficult conditions. How many kinds of weeds can you find on the sidewalks near your home?

Plantain is one of the most common sidewalk weeds. The tall spikes on this plant are clusters of tiny fruits which are eaten by many birds.

THE WHEAT GAME

Being a farmer has to be one of the world's greatest jobs!
You're outside in the sunshine all day, riding around on your tractor, wearing your most comfortable clothes.
You grow your own food, so you don't have to worry about going to the store.
As far as growing food is concerned, what could be easier?
All you have to do is plant a seed and watch it grow. Right? Not quite.

To get a better sense of what farming is really like, try playing The Wheat Game.

Wheat is the world's largest crop. One-seventh of all farm land around the world is used for growing wheat.

Here's your chance to see what farming is really like, and you don't even have to get dirty — or get any blisters.

BY MARY DONEV, STEF DONEV, AND CAROL GOLD

26. WEATHER ALE Roll die. Odd num heat damages pla move backward, even number, good rainfall move forward.

25. P ALER Roll o numbe locusts crop, m backward number, fe locusts, li damage, move forward.

24. RAIN DELAY: Too much rain slows growth. Next turn, roll even number to leave.

23. GOOD WEATHER Take ext turn.

RAIN: to 1 and ver

34. RAIN DELAY: Fields too muddy to harvest. Next turn, roll even number to leave.

35. EXTRA FARM HANDS HIRED Ahead 4.

36.

37. FARM HA QUITS: Back 1.

Start over from square 1.

39.

40. PREPARE TO MEET BUYER. Lose 1 turn.

41. SELLING A Odd number, pric move backward, even mber, good price, move ard.

NT ALERT. dd number, can't new truck to ship in, move backward, e number, can buy truc fo

44. RATS INF STORAGE SHED Lose 1 turn.

47. BUYER CANCELS ORDER Back to square

48. SHIPPING DELAY: Must roll e number to leave.

49.

50. WHEAT GROUND INTO FLOUR:

FLOUR xxx

9

START

RULES

Purpose
To plant your wheat and take it all the way through to the end, where it is ground into flour. The first player to do so wins.

Number of players
2 to 4

Equipment
One die and a marker for each person. You can use different colored beans or beads for markers.

Directions
Players take turns throwing the die, and move ahead the number of squares indicated, unless prevented by special instructions printed on a square.

1. READY FOR PLANTING: Roll even number to start game.

2.

3. RAIN DELAYS PLANTING: Lose 1 turn.

4.

5. WEATHER ALERT: Roll die. Odd number means late frost kills plants, move backward; even number, cloud cover prevents frost, move forward.

6.

7. PESTS EAT SEEDLINGS: Return to square 1 and start over.

8.

9. ADD FERTILIZER: Take extra turn.

10.

11.

12. HAIL DAMAGE: Next turn, roll even number to move.

13.

14.

15. WEATHER ALERT: Roll die. Odd number, hail kills plants, move backward; even number, storm misses, move forward.

16.

17. PLANT DISEASE INFECTS WHEAT: Back to square 9 but don't take the extra turn.

18.

19.

20.

21. Move forward to square 28.

28.

29.

30. PLANT DISEASE: Wheat turns black. Back to square 9 but don't take extra turn.

31. ORGANIZE HARVEST: Lose 1 turn.

32. EQUIPMENT ALERT: Roll die. Odd number, tractor broken, move backward; even number, tractor repaired, move forward.

33.

26. WEATHER ALERT: Roll die. Odd number, heat damages plants, move backward; even number, good rainfall, move forward.

25. PEST ALERT: Roll die. Odd number, many locusts eat crop, move backward; even number, few locusts, little damage, move forward.

24. RAIN DELAY: Too much rain slows growth. Next turn, roll even number to leave.

23. GOOD WEATHER: Take extra turn.

22. NO RAIN: Return to square 1 and start over.

34. RAIN DELAY: Fields too muddy to harvest. Next turn, roll even number to leave.

35. EXTRA FARM HANDS HIRED Ahead 4.

36.

37. FARM HAND QUITS: Back 1.

38. FIRE DESTROYS CROP: Start over from square 1.

39.

40. PREPARE TO MEET BUYER. Lose 1 turn.

50. WHEAT GROUND INTO FLOUR: Game over.

49.

48. SHIPPING DELAY: Must roll even number to leave.

47. BUYER CANCELS ORDER. Back to square 40.

46. RAIL STRIKE: Lose 1 turn.

45.

44. RATS INFEST STORAGE SHED. Lose 1 turn.

43. EQUIPMENT ALERT: Roll die. Odd number can't afford new truck to ship grain, move backward; even number, can buy truck, move forward.

42.

41. SELLING ALERT: Roll die. Odd number, price too low, move backward; even number, good price, move forward.

On ALERT squares, players throw the die. If an odd number is rolled, the player moves backward that number of squares. If an even number is rolled, the player moves forward that number of squares. When the players are sent back or ahead to a square that has special instructions on it (for instance, roll the die) the players must wait until the next turn to follow the instructions.

Up to two markers can be on a square at any one time. When a third marker lands on a square, all three players roll the die. The player who rolls the lowest number moves back that number. In case of a tie, all three players roll again.

FLASHBACK

Barbara McClintock was listening to the radio when she heard an amazing news item — she had just won the 1982 Nobel Prize for Medicine or Physiology. The prize was for work she had done 31 years before!

McClintock's area of science is called genetics (je-NET-iks). It's the study of how characteristics are passed on from parents to offspring. (You are your parents' offspring and geneticists could explain to you why you are like your parents in some important ways.)

In the late 1940s, McClintock began to work on a genetics problem. She noticed an unusual thing about Indian corn: like snowflakes, no two ears of corn were alike. Every ear was different. But a big idea in genetics at the time was that offspring are always like their parents in important ways. McClintock wanted to find out why so many differences were showing up.

Geneticists knew that chromosomes carried the information that determines how a human being or an ear of corn will look. And on each chromosome, thousands of genes carry specific instructions — such as "make black hair" or "make this corn kernel fat and juicy." They thought the genes were arranged in a set order that didn't change, like beads on

Jumping Genes

a string or pages in a book. And that in turn explained why offspring are like their parents.

McClintock saw that the big ideas of the day simply could not explain why each beautiful ear of corn was different from the next. She thought that there must be some genes that didn't follow the rules. She was right. Her research introduced scientists to a brand new big idea — jumping genes. She showed how certain genes were moving around and how this idea would make sense of the "Indian corn problem." Genes were not, after all, as straightforward as beads on a string.

McClintock's ideas were so amazing that other scientists didn't know what to do with them. Some even rejected her work. But she had faith in herself. She once said, "If you know you're right, you don't care. You know that sooner or later it will come out in the wash."

So far, every living thing studied has been shown to have jumping genes. Today, scientists are making Barbara McClintock's jumping genes jump. They use the jumpers to make corn sweeter, to help them search for cures for diseases, and to expand their knowledge of genetics.

DESIGNING Green

Do you ever wonder why your neighborhood park looks
so nice? I went looking for the answer by visiting
Donna Hinde. She is a landscape architect.

Hinde's office was filled with maps,
sketches, drawings, and plans.
She also had lots of books
about plants.

She explained to me that landscape architects
try to make outdoor spaces that look good
and are suited to their purposes.
They decide where sidewalks should go,
what kinds of lamps to use,
and how gardens should look.

BY MARGO BEGGS

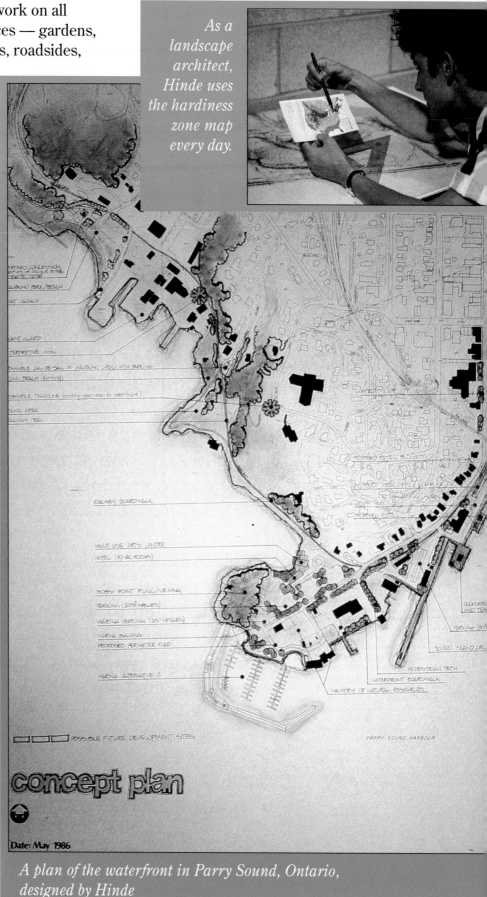

Landscape architects work on all kinds of outdoor spaces — gardens, office buildings, parks, roadsides, waterfronts, even zoos. Their most important tool? Plants!

"Plants look nice, provide shade, and offer privacy," says Hinde. "They also do other important jobs, such as help stop erosion, keep snow from blowing on roads, and prevent the wind from blowing people over. Grass, plants, and trees also help to cut down on noise by muffling it."

Hinde says that when she starts a new project, "the first thing I do is look at the space. I imagine how it should look when it's finished. Clean and modern? Wild and natural?" The plants she chooses will make all the difference.

Next she figures out what kinds of plants will grow there. "I use a special map that splits North America into hardiness zones. Plants need the right kind of climate — the right amount of rain and sun and the right temperatures — to grow well. This map helps me choose plants that will grow well in the zone where I'm working."

Hinde needs to spend time exploring the space. She finds out how much sun, wind, traffic, and maintenance the space will get. Finally, Hinde picks the plants she wants to

concept plan

Date: May 1986

A plan of the waterfront in Parry Sound, Ontario, designed by Hinde

14

use by asking herself more questions: "Should the plants have flowers? What color should the flowers be? Do we want lots of evergreens, or should there be plants that shed their leaves, called deciduous (de-SIJ-oo-us) plants?" Shade is great in the summer, but the extra light through the trees in the winter is very welcome.

When Hinde has made her decisions, she does sketches and then makes detailed plans. By following Hinde's plans, gardeners and other workers make the space look just the way she designed it.

Parry Sound waterfront before Hinde's work

Parry Sound waterfront after Hinde's work

What jobs are trees doing around your home or school? Do a sketch of a home or school you would build, and include all the trees and bushes you would plant. Why would you put them where you do?

CHECK IT OUT!

What grows best where you live? Libraries have gardening books full of colorful photographs and sketches. Visit a large plant nursery so you can see some of the plants that you might grow. Use a book, or ask someone at the nursery for help in starting a landscaping project at home.

The rafflesia is a plant with no stem or leaves. It's just a flower, and it's the largest in the world. It can grow to be over one metre across.

PLANT POWER

A landscape architect designed this plan to turn an unused piece of land into a great park. How? By using plant power!

If you wanted to create your own park, you could use plant power, too. Find a piece of land — even your own backyard will do — and sketch your own plan. Just follow these tips from landscape architect Donna Hinde.

1 Instead of ripping out weeds, or natural growth, why not put them to work? They'll be better for the park, and for the environment, than anything you could plant. That's because they won't need pesticides or extra water to grow well.

2 Try using ground covers instead of grass on some of the bare patches or hilly slopes. Rather than growing upward, these plants spread across the ground. They grow quickly and easily and, best of all, they don't need to be cut. You might try periwinkle, crown vetch, or forget-me-not. (But don't plant them where you'd like to play a game of softball!)

3 Use trees to create a wildlife area. Walnut and oak trees attract squirrels. Small animals like to snack on the bark of fruit trees. Junipers offer shelter for wildlife. Birds like the berries of the mountain ash and Russian olive.

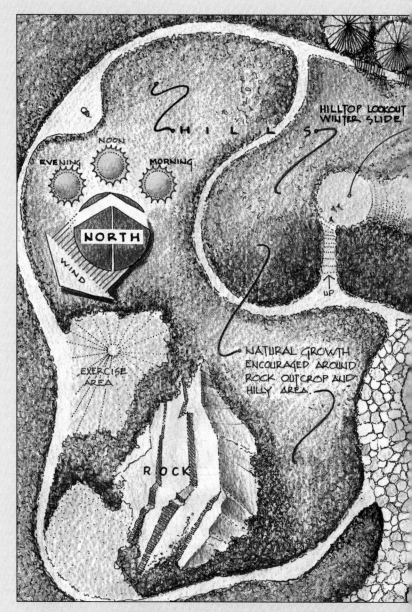

4 If you're planning your park during the summer, think ahead to the winter. Your park will look nice year-round if you choose your plants carefully. Many shrubs, like the red-twigged dogwood, have colorful branches. Bright holly berries will look pretty when you take a New Year's Day walk. And don't forget the springtime. Forsythia glow with yellow flowers in early spring. Most fruit trees burst with pink, purple, or white blossoms as the days get warmer.

5 Flowers make everyone happy. Dot your park with perennials — flowers that grow back every year. Irises in spring, daisies in summer, mums in the fall, and dozens of other flowers will make your park an ever-pleasing landscape.

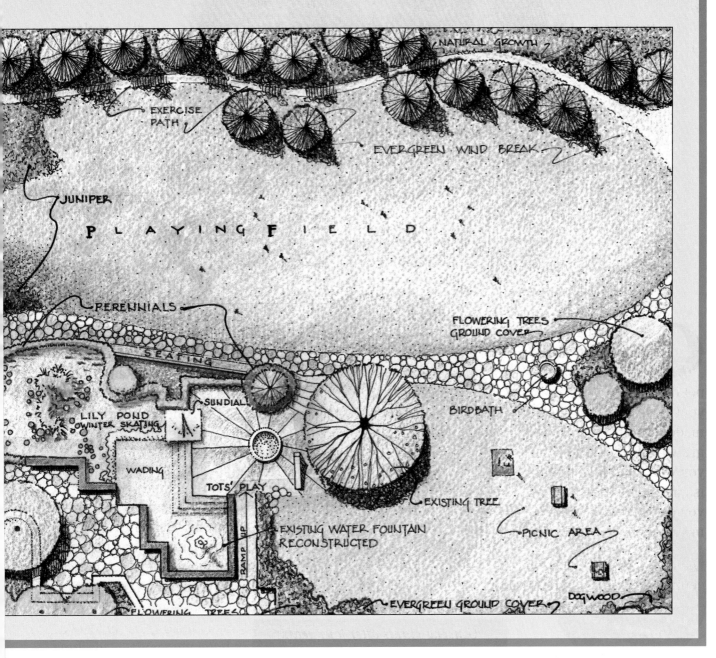

17

Kan-Shu: Is there a difference between Korean ginseng and North American ginseng?

Diana: We call the Korean ginseng red ginseng because of the way it is preserved. A special type of herb is wrapped around the root. When the root dries, it is red in color. It is used by the Chinese to purify the blood. What is grown in North America is called white ginseng and people use it when they feel tired or listless. The red ginseng is about 2000 years old, while the white ginseng is only 200 years old.

Kan-Shu: What should we look for when we buy ginseng?

Diana: You should look at the bulb — it's the most important part of the root. You look at the color and you feel the bulb to see if it's firm and strong.

Kan-Shu: Finally, where do you sell most of your ginseng?

Diana: We sell most of it to the countries in the Pacific rim.

Diana carefully chooses dried ginseng roots for export.

HARVEST OF HERBS

You can probably name dozens of plants that you eat. But there are also many plants that you put in your food to make it taste better. They are called herbs, and you probably eat them often without even knowing it. Take a look at these herbs that you might find in your garden — or on your dinner plate!

Lime mint grows well because insects hate it. And, just as you'd expect, it has a light taste of lime and mint. Try some in a tall glass of lemonade.

Mustard was originally used to hide the flavors of bad-tasting food. But these days, it's a real treat and comes in lots of varieties — yellow for your ballpark hot dog, deli-style for your lunch, and even flavors like strawberry and champagne. Mustard is made from crushed or ground mustard seed. You can grow it in your garden.

Mix the petals from these plants with a bit of mayonnaise for a nice lemony sauce for your vegetables at dinner. These "lemon gem" plants are closely related to the marigolds that you grow in your garden for decoration.

Dandelion

BY BARRIE. WATTS

How well do you know this familiar friend?

On sunny days,
the dandelion flowers open.
Each flower is at the end of a long stalk.
If you pick a dandelion, you can see that the stalk
is hollow like a straw.
Have you ever noticed the sticky,
white juice which comes out of the stalk?
It is food for the plant. If you get this juice
on your skin or your clothes,
it leaves brown marks.

A dandelion flower is made up of lots of tiny flowers growing very close together. This dandelion has been cut in half.

Inside each tiny flower there is some sweet juice called nectar. Wasps and other insects visit the dandelion because they eat the nectar.

The dandelion flower only stays open for a few days. Then it closes and the petals start to dry up and die. Tiny seeds begin to grow underneath the dried-up petals. They are soft and green. Each one has a tiny stalk growing from it, with soft white hairs at the top. Here you can see the flower a week later. The white tips are just showing. The green sepals around the flower keep the seeds safe until they are ripe.

When the seeds are fully grown, the dead petals drop off and the dandelion head opens again. In this photograph, the white hairs attached to the seeds are still damp and closed. You can't see the seeds yet. They are hidden inside.

When the seed head is half-open, as it is in this photograph, you can see the seeds. They have turned brown. The green sepals are folding back. Soon they will dry up and die.

The dandelion head has fully opened. It is as big as a golf ball. The outside is soft and fluffy. The white hairs have dried and opened into tiny parachutes. Each parachute is attached to one seed.

When the seeds are ripe, they are only loosely attached to the stalk. The wind lifts the parachutes up into the air and the seeds are blown away. Soon all the seeds have gone and the stalk is bare.

The seed is hard and has tiny hairs which act like hooks. It is very light. The seed is blown along by the wind. It can be carried a long way from the plant. If the seed lands on some soil, it may start to grow. From your experience, are dandelions successful at spreading their seeds around?

Here you can see a seed that has started to grow. It has grown roots and leaves. Can you see the parachute sticking up out of the soil next to the plant?

Conduct a popular opinion poll. Ask people of all ages what they think the difference is between a weed and a garden plant. Pick the answer you think is best, then ask your classmates to vote on whether they think it's true or false.

Discuss how you can find out what botanists think.

A year later, the dandelion plant is much bigger. On a sunny day, it blooms. And you know what happens next ...

The saguaro cactus is one of the world's tallest cacti. Some can grow as tall as 15 m.

25

A black fly hovers in the air over a strange-looking plant. Attracted by a sweet smell, the fly lands on the flat, reddish surface of one of the plant's leaves. It begins to crawl across. Suddenly, the leaf moves! Before the fly can get away, it's trapped — by a carnivorous, or meat-eating, plant.

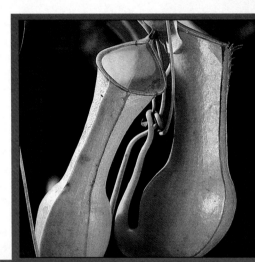

This is one type of pitcher plant. Some pitcher plants have one-way tunnels — once the insect is in, it has no way out!

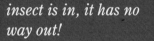

Probably the most famous of the carnivorous plants is the Venus flytrap. This plant is found in the swamps of North Carolina. The entire plant grows about 30 cm tall. In spring it has pretty white flowers blooming on top of tall stalks. But the most interesting parts of this plant are its leaves.

The flytrap's narrow green leaves grow in a circle around the plant's base. Each leaf blade opens into two halves, almost like a clamshell. The two halves, or lobes, are attached to a center rib. Each lobe is about two and a half centimetres in length. The inside surfaces of the lobes are usually a reddish color. Around the curved outer edge of each lobe is a row of stiff, pointed bristles, called cilia (SIL-ee-uh). On the inside surface of each lobe are three "trigger" hairs.

This sundew plant has a sticky substance on its leaves that traps animals.

You can see the reddish lobes and the cilia on this Venus flytrap's leaves.

Right: Here you can see the leaf of a Venus flytrap capturing a grasshopper.

d!

A MEAL IN THE LIFE OF A CARNIVOROUS PLANT

BY CYNTHIA OVERBECK

1 If you have a large tree by your home, then you know how great plants are for providing shade and keeping your house cool. What kind of cooling machine are these plants that lower the air temperature?

2 Careful planting of trees and bushes can protect crops from heavy rains or strong winds and so stop soil from eroding and blowing away. That means a bigger crop at harvest time. The plants are much nicer to look at than what unnatural protector?

3 When we cut down rain forests, we destroy a big area around them. The trees and plants absorb lots of water during heavy rains. Without these plants, flooding occurs, and once the water has drained away, the bare land dries rock hard. In a very short time, fertile rain forests can be replaced with barren deserts. What are those roots acting as?

4 Shhhh! Ever noticed the hush that surrounds you when you are in a forest? What machine are the trees and plants like when they absorb sound and bring noise down to a peaceful and healthy level?

5 You would probably be surprised by the number of birds and other animals that make plants their homes. Many animals also use trees to show off during mating season, for quick hiding places, for food, and much more. What are trees and other plants like when they provide such good housing?

6 Even after plants die, they continue to help the environment. As they are broken down by insects, bacteria, and so on, they are turned into rich, dark humus that improves the soil. What are plants acting as when they enrich the soil so it can support new plants?

**A. wind fencing   B. fertilizer
C. sponge   D. air conditioner
E. apartment building
F. muffler**

CUTTING EDGE

IT'S A PLANT, IT'S AN INSECT, IT'S A ...

It's hard to imagine plants with blue roots, leaves that glow in the dark, or a creature that's part wheat and part fish, but those are just some of the "plants" that now exist. Scientists have found

ways to change plant genes, or the plant's own instructions for how it will look and grow. This is called genetic engineering. It will let us create plants that can survive diseases, drought, weeds, herbicides, and much more. There is now a wheat plant that can survive freezing temperatures because scientists have given it genes from the flounder, a fish that can survive extreme cold.

But the most important thing genetic engineering might do is help feed our hungry world. Over one-third of the world's food crop is destroyed by pests each year. If scientists can develop crops that resist pests, then more people can be fed. Scientists may also be able to produce plants that can grow in soil where nothing grows now.

FLASHBACK

The Peanut Scientist

Cheese, milk, ink, soap, wood stain, insulating board — would you believe these can all be made with peanuts? They're just a few of the over 300 items that George Washington Carver produced using peanuts — and he changed agriculture in the southern United States forever.

Carver was born around 1864 in Missouri. He was extremely curious and had great instincts about plants. After university, he became head of the Department of Agriculture at Tuskegee Institute in Alabama. There he worked on the problem of enriching Alabama's soil. The land was tired out from the constant growing and harvesting of cotton, a crop that takes a lot of nutrients out of the soil, and leaves it too poor to grow other crops. But Carver found that peanuts could grow in the poor soil. They also helped make the land richer by using less nitrogen, an important soil nutrient. That meant more nitrogen could build up for other plants. But if he wanted farmers to grow peanuts, he had to show that there were lots of uses for peanuts — and he didn't stop until he had over 300 products! Peanuts became one of the top six crops in the United States, and Carver's work helped many farmers survive.

SOUNDS Great!

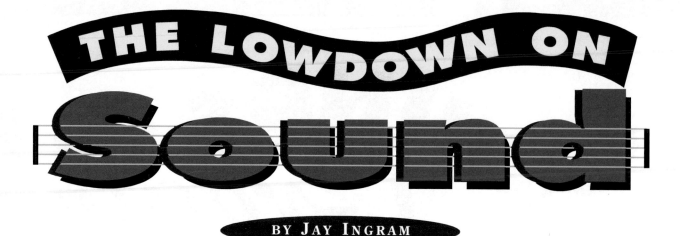

THE LOWDOWN ON Sound

BY JAY INGRAM

Sound is something that you can hear, right?
Well, that's partly true, but humans are
pretty limited in their hearing abilities
compared to other animals.
Both dogs and cats can hear much higher-
pitched sounds than we can, and bats
spend all their time listening to sounds
so high-pitched we have no idea
they're there.

one note

ven so, we have very sensitive ears for the sounds we can hear. We're very good at hearing high sounds: you barely have to touch one of the top keys on the piano to be able to hear it.

To play the highest sounds we can hear, you'd need a piano keyboard more than two octaves higher at the top — at least 17 or 18 white keys added. And because you hear best when you're young, you might be able to hear the top notes on a piano with even three extra octaves! But

one extra octave

two extra octaves

three extra octaves

your parents wouldn't hear a thing if you played the top notes on that piano. (Maybe they'd like to go out and buy one of those pianos right now!)

Even with this impressive hearing, there are lots of sounds around us that we just can't hear — even though some of them are really loud. Imagine being able to hear only sounds much lower than those you can hear now. What would it be like?

First of all, your ears would be much more sensitive to very deep sounds. The lowest note you can usually hear is not much lower than the bottom note on a piano. But that note wouldn't be low at all any more; it would be right about in the middle. You'd notice that you could hear things happening a lot farther away than you can now. That's because very low-pitched sounds — which are made of very long sound waves — can travel great distances. Long sound waves aren't stopped by buildings or hills because they just roll right over them. So you'd hear a thunderstorm from farther away than you can now.

But it could be even more dramatic than that. There are scientists who think that if you were in the middle of North America — in Winnipeg, Manitoba, or Kansas City, Kansas — you could hear the rumble of the waves hitting the shores of both the Atlantic and Pacific oceans! Goodbye peaceful prairies.

Cities would seem noisier, too. All the vibrations that you can only feel now, like that shuddering of the road when a truck or bus goes by, would become loud noises that you would certainly hear.

The Puerto Rican coqui (ko-KEE) frog makes a noise as loud as a roaring subway train.

But there'd be a lot you'd miss. The rustle of leaves in the forest, birds' songs, and most of the singing in the music you like, would be gone. Your breakfast cereal would be silent. You could eat potato chips in the library and there'd be no angry looks — there'd be no crunch!

But, of course, librarians wouldn't be able to tell anyone to be quiet — their voices couldn't be heard. Like them, you'd have a tough time talking to your friends. Much of our speech is in the middle range of our hearing — the middle and upper part of the piano — so you'd have to learn to read lips.

There could be an even more serious problem. Everything might be drowned out by the sounds of your own body! Sounds strange, doesn't it, but try this: stick your fingers in your ears gently and then clench your fists. Do you hear that low rumble? It's actually coming from the muscles in your hands and arms. You don't believe it? Try clenching your fists harder. The noise gets louder, because your muscles are working harder! Unless you actually provide a path for the sound by sticking your fingers in your ears, you can't usually hear those muscles. That's because we're not very good at hearing such low-pitched sounds. What if you could? You'd be walking around with your ears full of rumbles,

MY ACHIN' EARDRUMS!

You may have heard noise so loud you couldn't hear your friend talking beside you, but what about sound so loud it could bore holes through walls? It's possible! The loudest sound ever recorded was created in a NASA lab back in 1965. It was made during rocket testing and registered 210 db. That's loud enough to put holes in solid material — and to be heard over 160 km away! Ouch!

roars, and bangs coming from your jaws, your arms, your neck — you'd even be able to hear the vibrations of your head every time you took a step! After a while, the novelty of hearing only low sounds would wear off. You'd get pretty tired of struggling to hear what your friends were saying, and trying not to hear all the sounds coming from your own body. Maybe we can't hear as well as some other animals, but hearing just what a typical kid can hear isn't so bad after all. You might even decide to pass up hearing only high sounds. You would hardly be able to hear yourself think because of all the noise coming from bats, insects, and baby mice. So, maybe hearing the sounds you can hear is okay. Even if the next sound you hear is your brother or sister yelling at you, it could be worse.

USEFUL WORDS TO KNOW

Decibel A measure of how much energy a sound carries — how strong it is. A conversation is 60 decibels (db), a noisy restaurant is 70db, and live rock music is 120db.

Infrasound A sound below what humans can hear. Scientists have discovered that elephants communicate using low sounds that humans can't hear. Their low rumbles produce very long sound waves that can travel far across forests and grasslands.

Ultrasound A sound above what humans can hear. These very high sounds are used by bats, porpoises, and some kinds of insects to communicate.

CHECK IT OUT!

Visit a stereo store and talk to someone there about different stereos. Does the number of decibels make a difference to the price? To how good your music sounds?

FLASHBACK

Bell with Helen Keller

"Hoy, Hoy!"

If Alexander Graham Bell had his way, that's how everyone would answer the phone. Bell is best known today for inventing the telephone, but he always thought he would be remembered instead as a teacher of the hearing impaired.

Born in 1847 in Edinburgh, Scotland, Bell grew up in a family that had great interest in sound. His father taught speech to the hearing impaired, and Bell's mother became deaf when Bell was 12. In 1870, the Bells moved to Brantford, Ontario. Less than a year later, Bell headed to Boston to work at a school for hearing-impaired children.

Mr. Telephone

In Boston, Bell began experimenting with electricity and communication. Thomas A. Watson assisted him in making electrical parts for his various experiments. The two men originally began work on a sophisticated telegraph, but soon Bell became interested in the idea of transmitting speech.

One night in 1876, while experimenting, Bell spilled some battery acid on his pants. Without thinking, he called out "Mr. Watson, come here, I want you!" Watson came running into the room. He had heard every word on that first telephone!

ALL THE SOUNDS IN THE WORLD

BY JULIE WILLIAMS

**Do you remember learning to talk?
Most of us don't. When you were about
one year old, you probably started saying "ma ma"
and "da da" and maybe "up!" meaning "pick me up now!"
You learned more and more words until you were talking up
a storm. Your parents might say you've never stopped talking.**

Do you ever wonder what would have happened if you had been born in China, Mexico, or Egypt? You wouldn't have learned English as your native language, of course. But more than that, you wouldn't even make the same sounds when you speak as you do now.

When babies start babbling at about six months, they actually make every possible sound the human vocal tract is capable of making. They coo, they gurgle, they sing, they grunt, and they gasp. Interestingly, most of these "baby" sounds are found in one or more of the world's 4000 different languages.

!Kung children playing

For example, the French language has nasalized vowels, or sounds that pass through the spaces in the nose. The classic example is the phrase *un bon vin blanc.* English speakers can usually say these words correctly if they have a cold.

The !Kung people in the Kalahari desert of Africa have a click sound in their language.

The exclamation mark stands for the click. To say "!Kung," click your tongue against the top of your mouth as you say the word.

Ancient Hebrew and Arabic speakers closed the back part of their throats to make what is called a glottal stop.

French children in school

42

HEARING THE PRINTED WORD

What's the system that lets visually impaired people read? If you said Braille, you are partly right. Braille is an important tool. But this age of computers has come up with something even better for visually impaired readers — a machine that reads out loud.

The Kurzweil Reader at work

It's called the Kurzweil Personal Reader, and it reads any typewritten text, from schoolbooks to magazines. A scanner uses light to read the print, and the computer reads the print out loud. The system is also easy to carry — people never have to leave home without it!

It was part of the sound system of both Hebrew and Arabic in ancient times. To make this sound, say "uh" and stop the flow of air through your throat at the back.

Egyptian children

43

Some languages use tones, or musical pitches, to communicate meaning. Swedish and Chinese are two well-known examples. Listen closely to someone speaking one of these languages. To an English speaker it might sound like the person is singing. Languages may have as many as 12 different musical pitches — that's more than one octave.

The way people pronounce sounds within the same language can sometimes let you know where they live. Speakers of Castillian Spanish in Spain may sound like they are lisping when they

Chinese children having fun

A Spanish girl playing with her grandmother

pronounce words with the letter "c" followed by an "e" or an "i." A Castillian speaker says NATH-yon for the word *nacion*, meaning nation. A Latin American Spanish speaker says NAS-yon.

Why can babies make so many sounds, but you can't? Well for a few more years, you probably can. If you moved to Korea, you could probably learn to speak Korean just like a native. But after about the age of 12, you lose the ability to make those sounds. So you would be chatting in Korean sooner, and better, than your parents ever could!

THE musicMAKERS

Some people have to carry instruments as big as a tuba or cello in order to make music.

But musical insects are lucky — their "instruments" are built-in. They make music simply by playing different parts of their bodies.

BY PAMELA M. HICKMAN

Insect music is usually played by males that are trying to attract mates. Male crickets, however, also chirp to defend their territories. Scientists have discovered that all insects sing more slowly as the temperature drops. The snowy tree cricket has been called a "living thermometer" because of its very regular rate of chirping. In fact, if you count the number of chirps in eight seconds and add four, you'll have the approximate temperature in Celsius.

Cricket

Hey diddle diddle

A violin makes music when the bow is drawn over the strings. Some insects do this, too. They have a row of bumps known as a file and they have a scraper, which is a ridge or knob sticking out from part of their wings. The insect rubs the file and scraper together to produce a sound. Chirpers such as crickets and katydids make their music by rapidly rubbing the file (really a raised vein) on one wing against the scraper on another wing. Katydids may rub their wings together up to 50 million times in one summer!

45

Rum-pa-pum-pum

Male cicadas are the loudest of all insects, broadcasting up to 400 m away, especially on hot summer days. Cicadas are sometimes called hydro bugs because their buzzing noise sounds like the vibrations from heavy power lines or fluorescent lights. Their sound is produced from a pair of drum-like membranes (drumheads) on their abdomens. Inside the abdomen's air chamber is a group of muscles attached to the drumhead. By tightening the muscles, the drumhead is tensed, like pulling back on an elastic band. When the muscles are relaxed, the drumhead vibrates, hitting the inside of the abdomen's walls and producing the familiar sound.

Cicada

Tickers ...

You've heard of a haunted house, but what about a haunted chair or desk? Death-watch beetles burrow into wood and make a ticking sound by knocking their heads against the wood to call their mates.

Superstitious people believed that the ticking sound was a forewarning of death.

Death-watch beetle

Whiners and buzzers

Lie in a field on a warm summer's day with your eyes closed and you'll soon hear the sound of insects. Listen for the whining of mosquitoes and buzzing of bees. How do they make their sounds? The beating of their wings produces the music — the faster the wing beat, the higher the pitch. Which one do you think beats the fastest?

Bees and mosquitoes

. . . and clickers

Have you ever seen a beetle turned over on its back? It wiggles its legs in the air but can't get flipped over again. The click beetle is an exception. It has a built-in catapult. Its flexible body arches and then suddenly straightens up. As it straightens, a spine-like structure on its underside slides into a groove on its abdomen. Part way in, it catches on a knob in the groove. Once it slides past this knob, it clicks into the groove with such force, the beetle does a forward flip. If you are watching, you'll jump too, because it makes a loud click.

Click beetle

A catapulting click beetle in action

Try THIS

In Japan, some people keep cicadas and crickets in cages so they can listen to them sing. You can collect and keep an adult cricket in a jar in your own home. Put a wet sponge in the jar to give your temporary pet moisture and feed it ground-up dry dog food or chicken mash.

Be sure to punch holes in the jar's lid with a hammer and nail. Not only will you enjoy your cricket's serenades, but you will also be able to see how it makes its music. Be sure to return the cricket to its natural home in a few days.

CHECK IT OUT!

Whales sing to keep in touch with other whales in their pod, and they can communicate over great distances.

Look up your favorite animals in different encyclopedias. Find out how they use sound to communicate with one another.

PRESENTING THE MRobert Minden ENSEMBLE

What do a plastic drain pipe, a Slinky™, and a knitting needle have in common? They're all instruments used by the Robert Minden Ensemble!

Kirsty interviewing the ensemble

BY KIRSTY DICK

Kirsty: Where did you get the idea for the instruments?

Robert: It grew slowly. The first idea was playing music on the saw. Tom Scribner (an old vaudevillian saw player) came up with different ideas for sound by exploring where we live: the kitchen, the workplace, and the workroom. It started with hitting and striking things and listening to what they sounded like.

and stuff like that, but we had to become our own teachers. We've been learning how by listening to other musicians, listening and watching other performing groups, and listening to a lot of records.

Dewi: … and going to a lot of performances and seeing other kinds of theater music, and imagining how we could do that.

Robert, Dewi, Andrea, and Carla performing

Andrea with a collection of musical bottles

Kirsty: Did you have to train to be able to play the instruments?

Robert: You have to train yourself to do anything well. We didn't go to school to learn how to play things like the saw, mixing bowls,

Kirsty: Did you have to play real instruments before this?

Dewi: Well, we have all played other, more ordinary instruments before. I started on the piano and trumpet when I was little.

Andrea played the flute and recorder when she was young. But you don't have to start that way.

Robert: The man who taught me how to play the saw, Tom, didn't read music. He never played an instrument before he played the saw, and that's all he ever played. He started playing the saw because he loved the sound of it and just wanted to teach himself.

Kirsty: Are you the only group you know that uses these instruments?

Robert: No, there are lots of groups experimenting, making music on ordinary stuff, and even on garbage and junk. I do think that we're the only group that actually travels because it's really hard to travel ...

Dewi: ... because there's so much junk ...

Robert: ... and carry all this stuff. We travel with about 500 kg of instruments. So I think we're the only group that travels with so much junk.

Dewi: We're probably the only group like this that is actually on tour.

Kirsty: Where did you get the materials for the instruments?

Andrea: Well, we started finding the first ones right in our home. We played empty tin cans, kitchen bowls, and things like that. Then when we started composing for all these instruments, we needed more of them. A lot of

them were easy to find because they are things people throw away. We play bottles, so we can go to a recycling depot and gather a whole bunch of bottles. We can collect a lot of things that way.

Kirsty: Did you make any of the instruments yourselves?

Carla: Yes. Actually, we work with a fifth member of our group, Nancy Walker. She's a visual artist and acts as the designer for our

Above: Andrea and Dewi getting an instrument ready
Right: Here's another fabulous instrument!

show. She helps us design and even invents some of the instruments. One of them is called a "drone," and she makes it with elastic bands and wood, and sometimes corks. She stretches an elastic band across a piece of wood and turns it into an instrument that spins through the air. The spinning makes the elastic band vibrate, and that makes a sound.

Kirsty: How long does it take to make the instruments?

Robert: There's no answer to that question because we're always remaking them, we're reinventing them, reimagining them. Let's say we have a bunch of plumbing pipes, and we hit them, and they make a great sound. That's one part of making the instrument. Next, we have to figure out a way of holding it on stage. Then we have to figure out a way to travel with it. We have to design a case that will fit. Our inventing never stops. Sometimes we'll add something on or even change the whole instrument.

Kirsty: What made you want to do this?

Dewi: Who wouldn't want to do this? It's such a great thing to be able to do. Sometimes it feels like we're lucky to have places that want us to play, and that we can go out on a big tour. It's a really exciting thing to be doing!

Robert: You know, if you add it all together — if you love meeting people, and you love sound, and you love expressing it and taking a strange journey — that's what we do.

Try **THIS**

Invent instruments from unusual materials. Get together with a small group and form a band — and then go on a tour of the school!

Have friendly competitions between the bands in your classroom. Which sounds the funniest? Strangest? Which sounds the most in tune?

Kalyanaraman Swaminathan of Tamil Nadu, India, played his one-man band (which must include at least three instruments played at once) for 244 hours, from August 21, 1988 to September 1, 1988.

51

ZENGHO

The church bells you hear today might have been much better instruments if only the secrets of ancient Chinese bells hadn't been lost for 2000 years.

Now those secrets are being discovered, and scientists are finding out just how far behind our modern bells — and much of modern sound — are.

BY ELIZABETH MACLEOD

U YI'S CHIME

The Chinese bells are not the same shape as bells we usually see in the western world. Also, they have little knobs on them. This design helps each bell make two sounds.

The chime bells pictured here were discovered in 1978 in the tomb of Zenghou Yi, or the Marquis Yi of Zeng. He was a rich Chinese nobleman living in the fifth century B.C. The writing on the bells told scientists the main secret of the bells — that each bell can play two different notes.

The bells are oval, not round like modern bells. The oval shape and the 36 little bumps on the bells allow the bells to sound one note when a bell is hit on the side, and a different note when it is hit on the front.

Listening for oil

How could you tell if there was an oil field under your backyard? One way scientists use to find oil and gas is to listen for echoes from underground shock waves, made by setting off a small explosion a few metres below the surface. Scientists can identify different types of rock and other buried materials by the different patterns the reflected shock waves make.

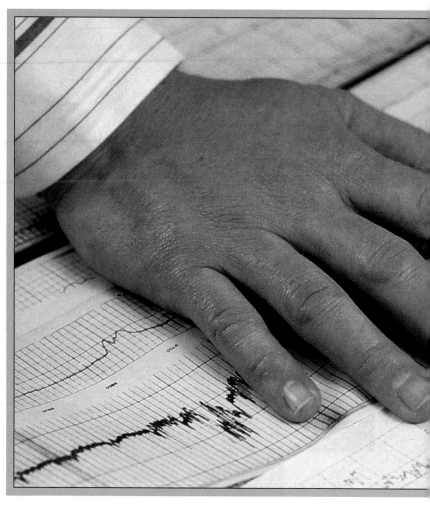

Sound dental care

Dentists can use ultrasound waves to clean teeth. They focus a beam of ultrasound waves onto the part they want to remove, such as tartar from teeth, or dead tissue from inside a decayed tooth. When the waves strike, the tartar or the dead tissue vibrates and shakes apart.

Unsound structures

A poorly made or worn-out railway track can break under stress and cause accidents. But engineers can find cracks, holes, and other unseen flaws inside solid metal structures by passing sound waves through them. The sound waves reflect back echoes from each flaw.

GREETINGS FROM EARTH

On Earth, sound energy is received by our radios and heard thanks to a speaker. But this energy also floats away from Earth toward other planets and stars, where it might be received, just as it is on Earth.

Scientists are excited about radio waves in space. They hope that somewhere someone might be receiving them. Since the 1960s, scientists have been

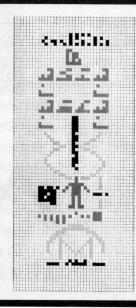

A message from Earth (right) was beamed from a radio telescope in 1974. When properly decoded, it describes our solar system (·····::···■), the radio telescope that sent the message (⋀), and what we look like (🧍).

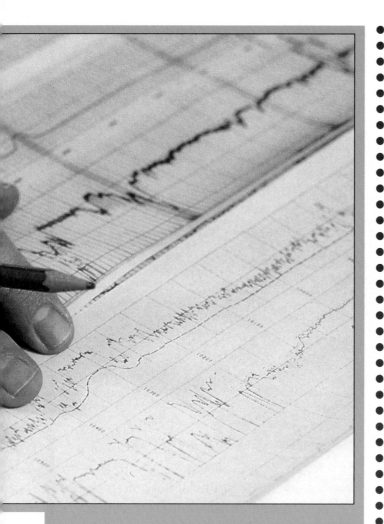

This printout shows the geologist what the sound waves hit underground. Now geologists can figure out where there might be oil.

You can use sound to tell how far away lightning is. During a thunderstorm, watch for lightning. Start counting as soon as you see it, and stop counting as soon as you hear the thunder. Divide that number by three, and that's how many kilometres the lightning is from you!

CHECK IT OUT!

If you could send a message to aliens, what would you want to tell them — using only sound — about planet Earth? Find out about the messages that were sent on the space probes Voyager 1 and 2. What would you have added to the record of sounds?

beaming messages to the rest of the universe via powerful radio instruments. Some of these messages show the position of Earth in the solar system. Others describe what human beings look like. This research is known as SETI — the Search for Extraterrestrial Intelligence.

Maybe one day scientists will receive a radio message back from space.

It might even say "Greetings!"

— Jessica Pegis

The island of Krakatoa, off southeast Asia, exploded in 1883. The sound was so loud that it was heard on more than one-tenth of the Earth's surface.

sfx!

Can you imagine a scary movie without creaking stairs, breaking glass, or eerie music? These are all sound effects — or to moviemakers and record producers, sfx. Here's how you can make some sound effects of your own. Choose a favorite story or poem and add some of these sound effects to it. You can even try recording your sfx creation!

BANG!

Thunder boom

Blow some air into a paper bag or balloon and pop it.

Forest fire

Crinkle up some cellophane. A little bit can sound like bacon frying, but a lot will sound like a whole forest is on fire.

Squishy footsteps

Fill a basin or bowl halfway with water. Soak dishcloths or washcloths in the water. Plop the soaked towels up and down in the water. It'll sound like someone trudging through the mud.

splish!

Rain

Sprinkle a few grains of uncooked rice or birdseed on your cookie sheet for raindrops. Drop a lot for a downpour!

Tidal wave

Go back to your basin of water. Make some loud splashes with your hands. (Make sure you're working in an area where it's okay to get wet!)

Clap of thunder

Hold the ends of a cookie sheet in your hands. (A big cookie sheet makes the best noise!) Give it one good hard shake to get a thundery noise.

SECRETS OF Survival

WHY WE WALK ON TWO LEGS

BY
JAY INGRAM

Baboons

What would it be like if you walked on all fours? First of all, you would have front feet instead of hands. You would spend a lot more money on shoes, but a lot less on gloves. A baseball glove would become a baseball "shoe." Skateboards would be okay, but it would be pretty hard to ride a bicycle! You would have to get a special one with four pedals and no handlebars. And you would have to get used to holding a pen or pencil between your toes ... your front toes.

It's hard to imagine walking around on all fours because our bodies aren't built for it. Even though we have exactly the same set of bones and muscles that horses, tigers, and elephants have, we humans have been walking upright for so long that our bodies are now completely remodeled for standing up. But don't take my word for it: check out your body from top to toe and you'll see just how different you are from our four-legged friends.

Horses

Start with your head. You would have a hard time walking on all fours with your head the way it is. It's angled so that you're looking straight out in front of you when you are standing up. That means if you were down on all fours, you would be staring into the ground a few centimetres in front of your feet. That's not very helpful if you have to run through a forest!

Your hands have changed, too. They're not strongly muscled for supporting your weight while you're running. You can't climb a tree as well as most monkeys, because your hand bones are no longer curved for gripping. But you can do something most animals can't. You can touch the tip of each finger with your thumb. That's called the opposable thumb, and we share this characteristic with monkeys and apes. Their hands are very muscular to support them while running or swinging through trees. Our hands aren't as strong, but we can make very precise movements. Have you ever seen an ape try to thread a needle?

Stand sideways and look at yourself in a full-length mirror. See how straight up and down you are? That makes it easy for you to balance when you're standing, because your

weight is pretty well centered along an imaginary line running from your head to your feet. But a chimpanzee is different. When it stands on two legs, it's in a "Z" shape, not a straight line. The center of its weight is much more forward because its shoulders and arms support its body weight as well as its legs and feet. It has to keep its muscles tense to balance on two feet, so it prefers to stay on all fours.

CUTTING EDGE

HELPING EARS TO READ ...

Money talks — at least it does in Canada. The Canadian Mint has printed bills that actually speak their value out loud. The talking money is designed to help visually impaired people.

The bills don't really talk — a pocket-sized electronic reader actually tells how much each piece of money is worth.

Here's how it works. A single bill is put into the battery-powered reader. At a touch of a button, the machine recognizes a pattern on the bill. Then, in a computer voice, the machine tells how much the bill is worth.

And now Canadians will really have something to bank on. More bills are soon expected to hit the streets ... talking.

— Elizabeth Vitton

Stay COOL!

BY RUSSELL GINNS

When the weather gets hot,
you have lots of different ways to keep cool.
You can fan yourself, you can go for a swim,
or you can crank up the air conditioner.

Animals need to stay cool, too. They have just as many ways as you do to make it through hot days.

Flapping its ears is never going to make this elephant fly. But it will stir up a nice, cool breeze!

A rabbit's long ears help it to hear better. But they also act as air conditioners. Blood carries around a lot of body heat. Some of that heat goes through the thin skin of the rabbit's ears and into the air.

A hippopotamus has eyes and a nose that stick out above its head. When it sinks the rest of its body underwater, it can see what's going on and still breathe.

When your dog pants, it doesn't always mean that it wants a drink of water. A dog sweats through its tongue. When sweat leaves a dog's body, it carries away lots of heat. When a dog pants, it's getting rid of more sweat and staying cool.

Try
THIS

Your body sweats to cool you down. Blow on your dry skin. Now wet your skin and blow on it again. Notice how it feels cooler the second time. The evaporation of moisture from your skin's surface takes heat away. Rubbing alcohol cools skin even better than water does because it evaporates faster.

CHECK IT OUT!

Why do some people faint or have giddy spells when the weather is hot? How do we help people recover from a faint? Ask your school nurse, a lifeguard, or a volunteer from the Red Cross.

Lions don't yawn because they're tired. They are testing the air for the smell of other animals.

FLASH**BACK**

Cool Trucking

Humans have adapted to the places where they live by changing the temperature in their homes. In very hot places, air conditioning is a lifesaver — and not only in homes.

In 1938, the owner of Werner Transportation Company was talking about a truckload of chickens that had gone bad before it reached the market. "Why can't someone make a machine that will keep the inside of a truck cool?" he wanted to know. One of the men he was talking to was Mr. Numero, the owner of a company that made equipment for movie theaters.

Numero joked to Werner that he could build him a refrigerator for his truck. A few weeks later, Numero found a shiny new truck in his parking lot — Werner had taken him seriously! Fred Jones worked for Numero. Not only did he want to help his boss, but he wanted to try out an idea he had. Jones had been thinking about making an air cooler for a car. When he saw the truck, he was ready to go to work. He finally came up with a light, small, strong unit that went at the front of the truck, above the cab. It worked!

The company that Jones and Numero formed still makes air conditioned trucks today.

CAMELS
Ships of the Desert

BY JOHN BONNETT WEXO

Camels have played an important part in the lives of many people for at least 4000 years. And this is because one-humped camels, known as dromedaries, have a wonderful ability to live in places like the Sahara desert where the climate is very hot and dry. There are some places in the Sahara where rain doesn't fall for months, or even years. Animals may have to walk long distances for many days to get water. There may be nothing to eat but dry twigs.

Most animals would die under these conditions, but camels seem to thrive on them. They are famous for being able to go without water for long periods of time. And camels can carry a heavy load and walk for many days under the hottest sun.

Until recently, camels were really the only way to cross the worst deserts on Earth. That's why they are known as "ships of the desert." Today, it is possible to travel to some places in the desert by car, or to fly there. But there are still places where there are no roads or airfields — and camels are the best way to go.

The strange-looking body of a dromedary is perfect for living in a hot and sandy desert. Almost every part of its body helps it to survive in places where few animals can live. The huge feet of camels walk on sand without sinking into it. A camel's foot can be as big as a large plate.

A dromedary

Desert winds often blow sand into the air. To protect their eyes, camels have long eyelashes that catch most of the sand. If some sand gets into an eye, camels have a special third eyelid to get it out. Like a windshield wiper on a car, this extra eyelid moves from side to side and wipes the sand away. The eyelid is very thin, so camels can see through it. In sandstorms, camels often close their extra eyelids and keep walking. You might say that a camel can find its way through a sandstorm with its eyes closed.

To keep sand from blowing into their noses, camels can shut their nostrils. When there is no sand blowing in the wind, a camel can open its nostrils and breathe through its nose. When the wind starts to whip up the sand, the camel just closes up its nose. Wouldn't it be fun if you could open and close your nose?

A camel's nose opening and closing

A camel's head has built-in sun visors to help keep the bright sunlight out of its eyes. There are broad ridges of bone above each eye. These stick out far enough to shield the eyes when the sun is overhead. The ears of a camel are small to make it harder for sand to get into them.

Long legs and long necks are a great advantage for dromedaries in the desert. The camels can raise their heads more than three and a half metres in the air. And they can see long distances in a flat desert. This makes it easier for them to find food and water.

Camels don't need to drink water as often as other animals because they can save, or conserve, water better than most animals. Camels have ways to keep from sweating too much. When the air temperature rises, a camel just lets its own body temperature rise as well.

Bactrian camels

CAMEL FACTS

- Camel hair is used by nomads to make clothes and tents.
- All desert tribes depend on camel meat and milk as an important part of their food supply.
- A camel can lose four times as much water as a human being — up to almost half of its body weight — and still keep going.

- In many places, camels are used in place of money.
- The hump is a place for storing fat, not water as some people once thought. Fat is a source of energy.
- Camels like to drink clean water, and they may even turn down a drink if the water is too dirty.
- Camels are plant-eating animals.

This way, the camel doesn't start to sweat until the air gets really hot — and this saves a lot of water.

Bactrian camels have two humps. They are also shorter than the dromedaries, and have heavier bodies. Bactrian camels can survive in the high, cold mountains in Asia, unlike dromedaries which live in flat, hot deserts. People and camels cooperate in the harsh world of the desert and the mountains of Asia. People feed and water camels. In return, camels help people by carrying heavy loads from place to place.

But camels can take care of themselves without people — they are well-suited to their environment. Actually, all animals are well-suited to the places they live. We notice camels because it's so hard for us to imagine surviving in the desert.

Try **THIS**

Why doesn't a camel's big foot sink into the sand? Take a pencil and push it into some sand. See how easily the narrow pencil goes in?

Now put a large coin under the pencil. Notice how the broad surface of the coin keeps the pencil from going in so easily.

Camels are the only desert animals that can carry heavy loads from place to place.

Masters
of
Disguise

Every butterfly is covered with millions of
scales — from the tip of its wings to the
bottom of its feet. Scales have many uses.
They help control body temperature, they give
butterflies their beautiful colors, and they
protect butterflies from predators.

BY BETH WAGNER BRUST

Birdwing butterfly, Malaysia

Butterfly larva, North America

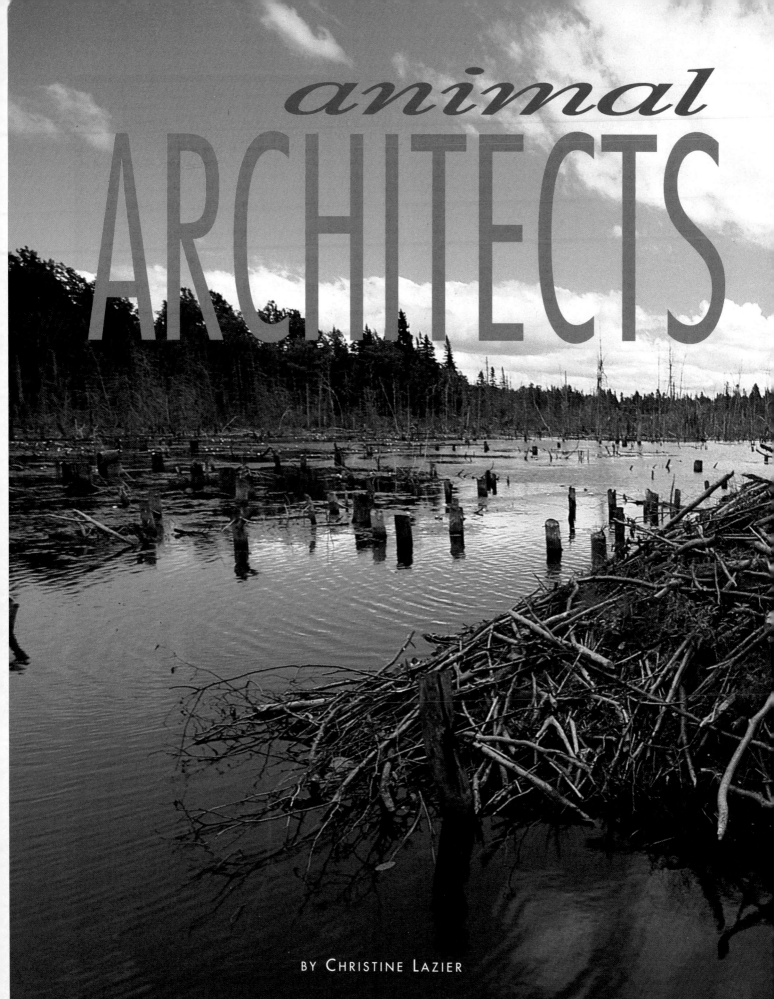

animal ARCHITECTS

BY CHRISTINE LAZIER

nimals build all sorts of different houses with different types of materials. Their houses protect them and their families from heat, cold, and danger. Rabbits dig an underground home called a burrow. Moles dig long tunnels under the earth. Monkeys and squirrels, like birds, prefer to make their homes in the trees. The homes beavers build on their dams are almost like palaces!

Beavers are swift and skillful swimmers, using their flat hands as paddles and their tails as rudders. They gnaw away, around and around a tree trunk until it is almost cut through, then pull and twist until it falls. They use the wood to build dams, and store the branches underwater as a food reserve for the winter. Once the dam is built, it's time to make a home. A beaver's home is called a lodge and it is made of woven sticks and mud.

Some monkeys and apes make nests. Chimpanzees make solid nests deep in the branches of trees. Large gorillas sleep in nests of grass and branches on the ground. The leaves and branches help to hide them while they sleep.

Above: Eagles carry big branches up into the mountains to build their huge nests

Right: Gorilla in the grass

the thread they move first across the space, then around and around to make the web. The strands which come straight out from the middle of the web are strong, but not sticky. The strands that go around the web are strong and very sticky! The moment one strand of the web is jerked, the spider rushes out to see what juicy bite has been caught in its delicate trap.

Above: Bees build perfect, regular cells of wax to make a home for their young.
Left: A spider spinning its web

Birds have only their feet and beaks to help them build nests. They collect grass or sticks and weave them together; they pick and pat bits of mud together; they peck out hollows and burrows. Once the nest is built, they line it with soft grass, feathers, or wool.

Many sea animals, such as oysters and mussels, feel at home in a shell. Instead of having their bones inside them, like we do, they have them outside. Their hard shells are their bones as well as their homes.

Spiders build strong, sticky webs to catch their food. Inside their bodies, spiders have a gland which makes a kind of silk. As they spin out

Gray squirrels peeking out of their tree stump home

SPACE • AGE

Space has always been an unfriendly environment to human beings. The lack of oxygen makes breathing impossible. Temperatures range from 100°C to –100°C.

Radiation and strong ultraviolet rays from the sun are deadly to human life. Very small, very fast-moving pieces of meteorites, called micrometeorites, are a further danger. They can actually dent the windows of a space shuttle.

Space shuttles are made to protect astronauts from these dangers. When an astronaut goes outside the space shuttle, the space suit has to offer the same protection. What does an astronaut wear before heading into space?

The astronaut first puts on a very special underwear. A series of tubes filled with water are woven into the fabric. The water in these tubes circulates continually. The water absorbs the heat given off by the astronaut. The heated water is cooled in a unit at the back of the underwear, and then recirculated over the astronaut's body. Without this water circulation, heat buildup inside the space suit would be unbearable.

Next, the astronaut slips on the bottom half of the space suit. The boots are attached directly to the pants.

The astronaut then puts on the upper part of the space suit which is made of stiff aluminum. A backpack attached to the back of the suit contains the astronaut's life-support system. It contains oxygen, a radio, a power pack, and the climate control system.

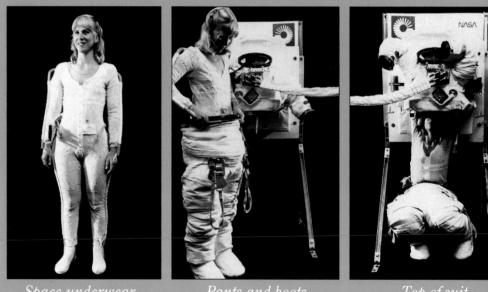

Space underwear   *Pants and boots*   *Top of suit*

The outer layers of the space suit are made up of several layers of fabric, plastic, and flexible metal. This outer "skin" is what protects the astronaut from harmful radiation and ultraviolet rays. Space suits also protect astronauts from the extremes in temperatures and from micrometeorites.

ARMOR

BY MARTIN TAQUET

Finally, the astronaut straps on a communications cap which contains two speakers and a microphone. Astronauts affectionately call it a Snoopy's cap.

Now come the gloves and the helmet. The helmet is made of a transparent plastic that is covered with a thin film of gold to block out solar radiation. The astronaut is now ready for space. She

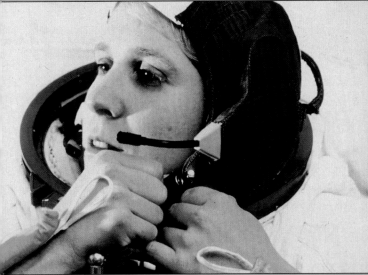

Snoopy's cap

enters the air lock, shuts the hatchway leading to the spaceship, and opens one leading to space. Air inside the air lock escapes with a whistle as the door opens.

The astronaut hooks on her safety line before venturing into the cargo hold of the shuttle. She is floating freely in space.

Safety line hook-up

THE ULTIMATE LIFELINE

In 1965, a Russian space traveler, or cosmonaut, named Alexei Leonov was attached to his spaceship by a hose. This tube provided Leonov with air to breathe, electricity to run the climate control system in his space suit, and his communications link.

Today, cosmonauts and astronauts carry all they need to be comfortable —

oxygen, an electrical system, and a radio — in one handy backpack.

The American astronauts even have a flying chair for propelling them away from the spaceship to pick up satellites for repair.

They call their flying chair the "space scooter."

CHECK IT OUT! Find out about the training that astronauts need to go through to help them adapt to conditions in outer space. You will probably get information by writing to the Canadian Space Agency or NASA.

The planet Earth has its own "space suit" — the atmosphere. It's a layer of gas, dust, and water vapor that holds in heat energy from the sun and filters out harmful ultraviolet rays.

Operation CLEAN Up

WHAT'S AHEAD

Even melting isn't a problem. The wood chips make the ice much less easy to melt, as Pyke demonstrated to the man who was then the Prime Minister of England, Winston Churchill. Pyke ran upstairs to Churchill's bathroom, where the Prime Minister was having a bath, dropped a cube of pycrete in, and the two of them watched as it floated in the hot bath, hardly melting at all. The plan with a big ship was to have cardboard tubes frozen into the hull from end to end — like veins — carrying ice-cold air through the ice to prevent it from melting in warm weather.

It's unfortunate that a great idea like giant ships made of pycrete had to come about because of a war. It would be so much more fun to think of taking a cruise on an ice ship!

You could even go island-hopping in the Caribbean. But Pyke dreamed them up because he thought they would be useful in an attack against enemy ports, and the war ended before any ice ships actually sailed. (There was one small version built in 1943 that sat for the summer in a lake in Ontario.)

Will we ever see pycrete ships on the oceans? Who knows? It's a lot cheaper and takes a lot less energy to turn sea water into ice than it does to turn iron into steel. But somehow, the idea of pycrete ships never took off. Maybe one day it will. And then maybe we'll look back and say, "Why didn't they build pycrete ships earlier?"

CHECK IT OUT!

Build an ice-block boat. Can you make one out of saltwater? Try to make your own pycrete and build a boat with it. Compare your ice boat to your pycrete boat. Which is stronger? Which floats better?

North Americans throw out about 20 000 televisions every day. If you stacked all the TVs we've thrown out on top of each other, they would reach almost as high as Mt. Everest.

THROWAWAY LIVING
IN THE 1950s

It's hard to imagine only 10 years between conserving

everything — even sawdust — in the 1940s

to throwing it all away in the 1950s.

LIFE magazine celebrated the thrill of being able

to toss out trays, plates, knives, and forks

with this trick photo, published in 1955.

ALL RECYCLABLES
INCLUDING NEWSPAPER

COMPOST

GARBAGE ... AND UNGARBAGE

Do you know the difference?

This dump is a mess! A lot of things in it are definitely not garbage. Can you find them all? Make a list of all the garbage and ungarbage you can identify, then write down where you think each piece really belongs.

Garbage is something that people use once or twice then throw away. Garbage is everything human-made that can't be recycled. Garbage takes up lots of room. It takes a long, long time to break down into the gases and chemicals it's made of. Plastic garbage can take as long as 450 years to break down. As it does, it lets off harmful chemicals into the soil, air, and water. If the pioneers had six-packs of soda, we would still have the plastic rings from them today.

A lot of things we think of as garbage are not. They are ungarbage. Ungarbage is everything that's natural and organic. Ungarbage breaks down quickly in sunlight and air and does not let off harmful gases or chemicals. Some ungarbage, like apple cores and banana peels, takes less than a year to break down. And when ungarbage breaks down it becomes dark, rich dirt called compost that's great for gardens. Find out how by reading "A Rotten Story" on the next page!

A ROTTEN STORY

So what really happens to garbage? If you keep a trash bag hanging around your kitchen too long in the summer you will know. Those smells come from rotting food scraps. Rotting is caused by the activity of millions of microbes — mostly fungi and bacteria. They live by eating the complex natural chemicals that are found in all foods. They break these chemicals down into simpler ones, and, as they do, they give off smelly gases such as methane and hydrogen sulfide. They are often helped by bigger creatures such as insects, worms, and mites.

— Evan and Janet Hadingham

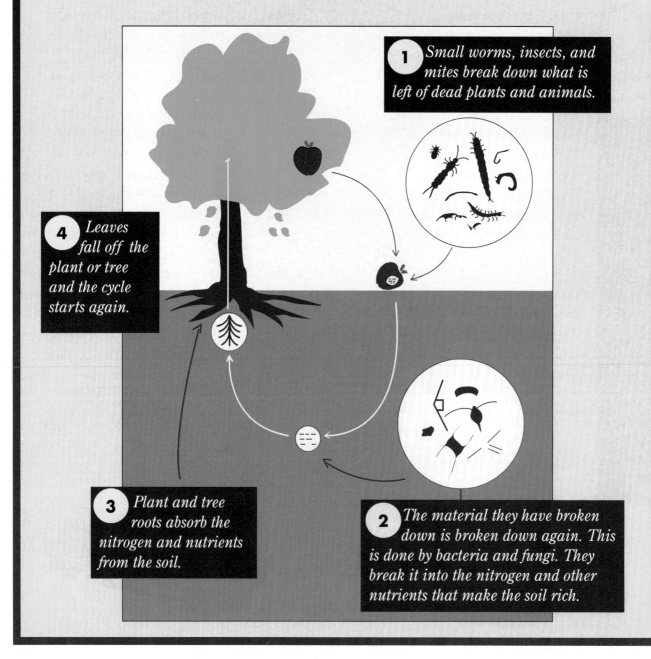

1 Small worms, insects, and mites break down what is left of dead plants and animals.

4 Leaves fall off the plant or tree and the cycle starts again.

3 Plant and tree roots absorb the nitrogen and nutrients from the soil.

2 The material they have broken down is broken down again. This is done by bacteria and fungi. They break it into the nitrogen and other nutrients that make the soil rich.

DOWN IN THE DUMPS

BY CHARLOTTE WILCOX

What happens to trash after trucks take it away? Most of it is taken to special areas called landfills. There are about 18 000 landfills in North America today.

A truck with another load

A landfill starts as a large hole in the ground, usually several hectares in size. Trucks drive into the hole and dump their trash. Then each layer of trash is covered with about 15 cm of dirt. Every day, more trash and another layer of dirt are added.

After a few years, the hole is filled and becomes level with the ground. After many years, the landfill grows higher and higher and becomes a hill of earth and trash.

The layers of earth and trash must always be packed down and leveled so that trucks can drive over the landfill. New trash must be covered with dirt as soon as possible to keep away animals and insects.

Huge bulldozers level the trash and pack it down. Some have giant spikes on their treads that break the trash into smaller pieces so it will pack better.

Giant graders take dirt from other parts of the landfill and spread it over the garbage. Then bulldozers pack the layers down.

The first landfills were called open dumps. Trash was simply hauled to a hole and dumped. The garbage was covered with earth only once in a while.

Open dumps can still be found, but most communities have stopped using them because open dumps cause many problems. They are even against the law in many areas.

An open pit garbage dump in Spain

CHECK IT OUT!

Find out from your garbage hauler where your trash goes. How near is the landfill to your house? Is the landfill a sanitary landfill? When was it built?

About one-third of your garbage is packaging that you throw out immediately.

Animals, insects, and fires are always problems at an open dump, but what's worse is how the water near and underneath the dump is affected.

When it rains, chemicals from the landfill run off into nearby lakes and streams, where they can harm fish and plants.

We have to respect and protect our land, and we also have to do the same for our air.

Do this simple experiment to find out how much air pollution there is in your neighborhood.

Take some index cards and spread a thin layer of petroleum jelly across one side of each one. Find some places where you can leave the cards for a week. You might hang them from branches or railings, or tape them to windows. Put some near a garage. Tape one to a kitchen or schoolroom wall. (You will have to leave part of the card clean so the tape will stick to it.) At the end of one week, collect the cards. Whatever has stuck to them is a record of the week's visible air pollution in that place. Place the petroleum jelly on a slide and get a closer look under the microscope.

— Betty Miles

The garbage sitting in an open dump begins to rot and turn into liquid. This liquid is called leachate (LEECH-ate), and it contains many harmful chemicals.

Rain drains through the rotting trash and soaks into the soil of the landfill. As the rain soaks deeper into the ground, some of the leachate goes with it. Finally the leachate reaches pockets of water, called groundwater, deep under the surface. These pockets of water are sometimes tapped by wells to provide drinking water for homes. When leachate gets into groundwater, it can make the water harmful and unusable.

Modern landfills, called sanitary landfills, are made to keep leachate from leaking into the soil and groundwater. Some landfills are covered on the bottom and sides with a layer of heavy clay soil that is too dense for the leachate to soak through.

Others are lined with large, heavy plastic sheets that trap the leachate and keep it from soaking into the water below. The plastic is made to remain strong and leakproof for many years after the landfill is closed.

This is a modern landfill in Arizona. In the background, a newly dug hole is ready to be filled with trash. Huge sheets of plastic are stretched over the hole's sides to collect leachate.

Landfills are used to handle all the solid waste in most areas. But landfills are not always the best way to get rid of garbage, especially in big cities. They cover large areas of land that are needed for other reasons. As landfills become full, new ones must be started, taking up more and more land for our trash.

"I" IS FOR INCINERATOR

You know about landfills. You know that they are crowded. You know that many are full, and now you know that many are dangerous. And you know that there is too much trash. So why don't we just burn the trash? Well, we do. We burn it in incinerators. It seems like a great idea — burning turns 10 cans of garbage into one can!

But when garbage is burned, it lets dangerous gases into the air. Things that were safe when we used them — like paper, plastic, and metal — become a health hazard when they are burned. Things that are hazardous wastes, such as oil, paint, or batteries, are even worse when they are burned.

Most of this material stays inside the incinerator. But some always escapes. It adds to acid rain and to smog. It lets poisons into the air, and those poisons land on fields and gardens and can get into our food.

So now we're back to square one. We can't let incinerators reduce garbage for us — we have to learn to reduce it ourselves.

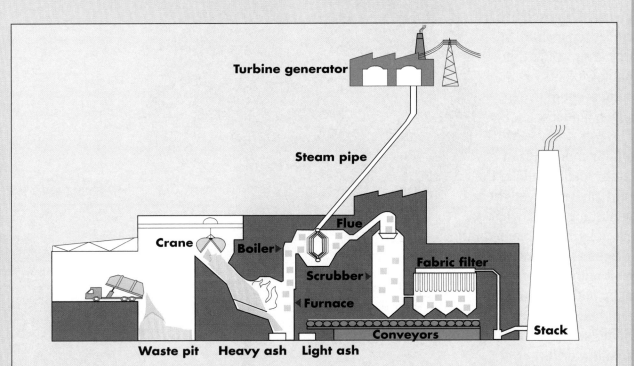

Trucks bring trash to the incinerator. They dump the trash into a pit, and cranes lift it into the furnace. It's burned at very high temperatures, and the heat it makes can be turned into steam to create electricity. (When the trash burns, heavy ash falls to the bottom of the pit. It is collected and taken away.) Smoke and gases go through a scrubber to get rid of dangerous chemicals. Any leftover ashes are caught in a fabric filter. Light ash is then collected. The gases that are left go up the smokestack.

THE LAND *of*
Frozen *Trash*

BY EVAN AND JANET HADINGHAM

Greenland sounds like a green and pleasant land. In reality, Greenland is so far north that it is mostly covered with a thick ice cap all year round. Even along the coast, the soil is bare and frozen as hard as rock. You would think that few plants or animals could live in such a landscape.

Yet, for thousands of years, small bands of the Inuit have survived there by hunting seals, whales, and polar bears. Some of their villages are so remote that until one hundred years ago, many of the Greenland Inuit had never seen a sailing ship nor had any other contact with the outside world.

You can see Greenland at the top of the world.

In the old days, there was no such thing as garbage for these hunters. Families often went hungry and sometimes even died from starvation, so everything the sea provided was precious. Since no trees grow there, the scraps of driftwood that washed up on the shore were carefully saved to make tools, bowls, plates,

96

and masks. And once a seal was speared, dragged home, and cooked, almost nothing of the animal was thrown away.

The meat was the most important part, but the Inuit found uses for all other parts of the seal, too. Its skin was used for clothes and bags. Its fat was eaten like butter, burned in lamps, and rubbed into the skin to protect it from the biting wind. Its long, twisting intestines were dried and stuffed with meat to make sausages. Its bones were carved into tools and toys.

Even its whiskers were saved and used as toothpicks. And they never had to think about how to get rid of the few scraps left over. Half-starved dogs and foxes snapped up every last bit tossed out the door.

About a hundred years ago, the lives of the people slowly began to change. Ships found their way through the pack ice and brought cans of whale meat, tea, sugar, and soda. Families no longer starved and didn't need to keep every scrap of material.

A village in eastern Greenland today

Life has become easier, but many of the Inuit's habits have stayed the same. Most villagers still throw the remains of meals out their doors and windows. The big difference is that dogs can't eat paper, plastic, and cans.

If you walk through a typical village in eastern Greenland today, perhaps the most impressive sight you'll see is the garbage mound. That's where the Inuit toss old rubber boots and tires, pieces of wooden crates, and thousands of cans. All this garbage usually lies in a giant heap in the center of the village, sometimes piled up higher than the rooftops of the houses.

The people don't seem to mind living with their trash. In fact, they've never had to think of trash as something ugly or dangerous. Microbes and bacteria can't grow in the cold, so the garbage heaps don't smell or spread disease. In any case, there's not much choice besides throwing the

Today, few spots are left anywhere in the world where you can't find a bottle top, an empty soda can, or some other kind of garbage. And even though most of us live differently from the people of eastern Greenland, in some ways we're very similar. Like them, our thinking hasn't changed much.

Many animals, like this polar bear, have grown to depend on garbage for survival.

garbage in the sea. It's nearly impossible to dig a hole or bury anything in the rock-hard ground.

In the far north, the cold, dry air prevents nearly all garbage from decaying. A candy wrapper dropped today will look much the same twenty years from now. Plastic bags snatched from dumps by high winds can be found hundreds of kilometres from the nearest house.

Most of us still throw out our trash without stopping to think who will take care of it or where it will end up. The only difference is that we don't usually see piles of thrown-out plastic, glass, paper, and metal outside our own front door.

More than six billion kilograms of trash are dumped into the sea every year.

Boy Tackles
Environmental Disaster
with Science

Imagine you come up with an idea for a science experiment, test it out, and find out that you have discovered a major environmental disaster.

That's what happened to David Grassby — and now this kid has oil company presidents listening to him!

BY SUSAN BERG

Susan: What did you want to discover?

David: I wanted to find out how much oil was left in a one-litre container after it was emptied to change a car's oil.

Susan: How did you think of that idea?

David: I guess it all started when I was over at a friend's house. I heard his dad in the garage saying that he couldn't get all the oil out of the container.

Susan: How did you do your experiment?

David: I phoned a few oil companies just to get some information on how much motor oil is sold every year. I phoned several gas stations. I averaged out all the numbers and found out that there were about 132 000 000 of those one-litre containers sold in Canada every year. I collected 100 of the containers and drained each one on top of a graduated cylinder for two minutes at around room temperature. There was an average of about 37 mL left in every container.

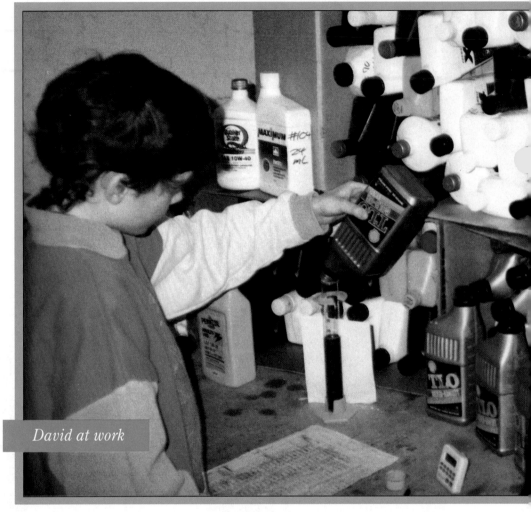

David at work

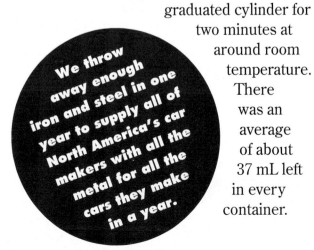

We throw away enough iron and steel in one year to supply all of North America's car makers with all the metal for all the cars they make in a year.

Susan: What was your conclusion?

David: If you multiply that 37 mL by the 132 000 000 containers, it comes out to almost 5 000 000 L of new, unused motor oil being dumped into Canadian landfills every year. That's like 85 fully loaded railway tank cars dumping their whole load into the ground. If you hear about one tank car going off the track it's a big disaster — but without knowing it, we have 85!

Susan: What was your solution?

David: I had two solutions. One was that motor oil be pumped the same way as gas is. The other was that customers use a refillable one-litre container.

Susan: What was your next step?

David: I wrote letters to some oil companies — Shell, Sunoco, Petro-Canada, and Imperial Oil. I also wrote some letters to the media to get more attention for the subject, and to the Minister of the Environment for Ontario.

Susan: What kind of response did you get?

David: The Minister did not write me back, but I did get good responses from Esso Petroleum Canada and Petro-Canada. Esso invited me to head office to speak with the president. Petro-Canada is going to give me a tour of its refinery.

Susan: Did you go to Esso?

David: Yes. I told the people there what I had found. They said that my numbers were 100 percent right.

Susan: What did they think of your solutions?

David: The president at Esso said a pump would not be worth the money because there are so many different kinds of motor oil. I showed him an article that I had read in the *Toronto Star* that said that most people preferred 5W30 — 90 percent of motor oil used is 5W30 and the other 10 percent is 10W30. After that, everybody got quiet and they really started to listen. They knew that there was no way out. They would have to deal with the problem.

Susan: What do you plan to do now?

David: I'm going to write another letter to the Minister of the Environment because I'm surprised that she did not respond. The government says it wants to cut down on packaging, and this is a very simple way. I will also wait for feedback to my other letters, find out what other companies plan to do in the future, and monitor what I have already done.

CUTTING
EDGE

HEAVY METAL

Measuring the amount of heavy metal pollution in our water can be tricky. Many metals won't stick together well in water. That means that scientists can't find out just how much of those metals are in the water.

But hydrologists, or scientists who study water, may have found a natural way to test metal levels. Barbara Scudder and Harry Leland have

The water hyacinth

discovered that water hyacinths in California's San Joaquin River can hold very high levels of metal pollution in the tips of their roots — and still look lovely. Scudder thinks that the hyacinths can be used to check for metals that are "hiding" in the water. A natural pollution meter!

FLASHBACK

Saving the Earth

If you're a kid with an interest in nature, where can it take you? For Rachel Carson, it led to a career that changed the way we look at the environment. In 1962, Carson wrote *Silent Spring*. This book shocked people when it described how we were poisoning animals by using pesticides on our crops. The book's title describes how Carson thought spring would sound if we kept ignoring what our chemicals were doing. Because of her book, the deadly chemical DDT was banned and people everywhere began to realize how everything we do affects the environment.

Carson was born in 1907. At university she studied zoology, or the science of animals, and became a writer for the U.S. Bureau of Fisheries. She was one of the first women to work there in a scientific position. She wrote four books, each about our dependence on natural processes. Although she died in 1964, her writing continues to influence us.

CHECK IT OUT!

Visit a home for the aged with some friends or your class. Talk to the residents and find out about the way they lived. What were some of their tricks for reducing and reusing?

The Netherlands has 15 000 km of bike paths. In China, there are 540 bicycles for every car.

M⬤ving Parts

Perpetual Motion

BY JAY INGRAM

Wouldn't it be great if you could really get something for nothing? A free ice-cream cone with every hamburger? The problem is there's hardly ever anything that's really free — you probably even pay for that ice-cream cone in the price of your hamburger.

But for hundreds of years, inventors have been trying to figure out how to get the ultimate free treat: a machine that will run forever without needing to have any fuel put in it. A perpetual motion machine.

Start a perpetual motion machine, and it would never stop. If the swings in the playground were perpetual motion machines, you could give me a careless little push just before you went home for dinner, and I would still be swinging the next morning, and the next week, and even the next year.

But scientists don't think it can be done. In fact, they'll laugh out loud at the idea of a perpetual motion machine. They're absolutely sure that the laws of nature won't allow it. And so far they're right — no one has ever

A traditional waterwheel at work in a mill on the road to Neukirch, Germany. This is how a waterwheel is normally used — water turns the wheel to provide power to run the mill. The wheel needs flowing water, like this river.

MACHINES

invented a machine that'll run forever ... on nothing. But some of the designs for perpetual motion machines look pretty good. They look like they should work, and you have to be pretty clever to figure out why they don't.

Here's a perfect example, from a long time ago — the year 1618 to be exact. It's a mill for grinding grain, but this one's different from most other mills. Most mills were built beside streams or rivers so they could use the flowing water to turn the millwheel. Instead this mill uses the same water, over and over again. You could put this mill in the desert, get it going, and just let it run. At least that's what the inventor, Robert Fludd, thought.

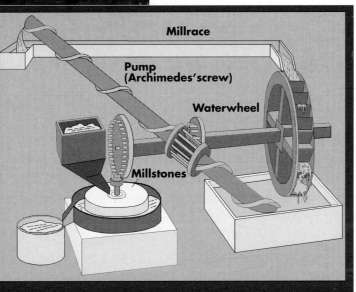

Robert Fludd's perpetual motion machine: Water runs along the top of the mill and falls, turning the wheel. The wheel turns the screw-shaped tube. The tube is supposed to lift the water up to the top. The water is supposed to run along the top and then start all over again. Do you think it works?

Watch where the water goes, and you'll see how it's supposed to work. It runs along the top of the mill, then falls, turning the waterwheel as it does. This wheel not only turns the mill to grind the grain, it also turns that long, spiral, screw-shaped tube in the middle. The tube is supposed to lift the water back up to the top. It then runs along the top of the mill, and starts the whole cycle again. Simple, right? Just add water, and grind all the grain you can get. But it won't work. Why?

The big problem here is that you'd need all the energy from the falling water just to lift the water back up again, so there wouldn't be anything left over to run the mill. There's another catch, too: no machine is perfect. All the wheels and gears in this invention rub against each other when they turn. That friction changes some of the water's energy into heat — just like you can make your hands hot by rubbing your palms together. But once that energy is turned to heat, it can't be used to turn wheels. As soon as energy is lost like this, this perpetual mill will grind to a halt.

How about this very simple idea for perpetual motion: a very powerful magnet at the top of a ramp pulls a ball all the way up from the bottom. But at the last second, the ball falls through a hole in the ramp, rolls back to the bottom, then starts climbing again. Once you let the ball go, it goes ... and goes ... and goes.

The magnet pulls the ball up the ramp.
The ball falls through the hole
and rolls back to the bottom of the ramp.
This machine is supposed
to keep on going — but does it?

But there is one slight problem. If this magnet were strong enough to pull the ball all the way from the bottom, there's no way the ball would be able to fall through the hole. The magnet would just pull it right over the hole, the ball would smack into the magnet, and that would be that.

It's funny ... there are two kinds of perpetual motion machines. There are those like the ones here that look good but don't work. Then there are machines that do work, but only because there's a trick — some hidden source of power that is supposed to fool people into thinking the machine really is a perpetual motion device. But there are still inventors who claim they've finally done what hundreds before them have failed to do — build a machine that will run forever, without any power. And if they offer to sell it to you? You're better off saving your money for that free ice-cream cone!

CHECK IT OUT!

Alfred Clark loved to rock in his rocking chair. And he loved butter. But in 1913, when he lived, you had to make your own butter by churning cream. Clark didn't like doing that. So he invented the Rocking Chair Butter Churn. First you poured cream into a barrel attached to the chair. Then you sat and rocked. After a while — a long while — the cream became butter.

Do research about other wild inventions. What can you find out about wacky alarm clocks? Or portable showers?

THE PROOF IS IN THE PATENT

Eureka! You have just come up with a fantastic new invention: a bicycle helmet for fish, or maybe an automatic shoelace-tying machine. You're a genius! But what should you do with your idea?

You could build your amazing invention and use it around your house. Or you could show it off to your friends. But what if it's a really great invention and you are convinced no one should be without it? If you think your idea is the latest greatest discovery — like the light bulb or the airplane — you might want to do what thousands of inventors do every week: apply for a patent.

A patent is a piece of paper that proves that an idea is yours. When you patent something, anyone else who uses your idea has to share the profits with you.

So how can you get a patent for your fish helmet? The first step is to make sure that someone has not already invented it. To do that, you will have to go to the search room in your national patent office.

Once you are sure that you are the first person to invent a fish helmet, then you can apply for a patent. You will have to draw your invention and describe what it does and how it works. Then the application goes to the experts — the patent examiners. Each examiner is an expert on a few topics. Together, they have to know about everything from potato peelers to chemistry!

An examiner will give an inventor a patent if two things are true about the invention. It must be original — no one has patented it before — and it has to work.

Some inventions don't work, and they don't get patents. Fewer than five percent of all patents wind up being used or sold. But getting a patent isn't the main reason to think up inventions. It's really all about being creative. And your fish will still love its new bicycle helmet.

— Russell Ginns

The Simplest Machine

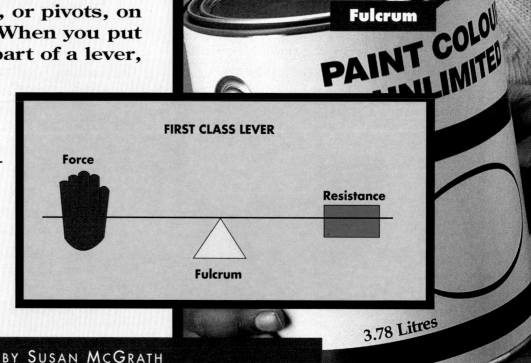

Resistance

Fulcrum

PAINT COLOUR UNLIMITED

3.78 Litres

I f someone said "Quick! Name a machine!" you might shout "Lawn mower!" You probably would not cry "Lever!" People usually think of a machine as anything with a motor. But physicists (FI-zi-sists) define a machine as anything that does work.

Work is done when something is moved by a force. A machine is a thing used to move something else. A lever is one kind of machine. It consists of a bar that turns, or pivots, on a fixed point. When you put force on one part of a lever, another part of it moves something. We see levers everywhere — at home and at play.

FIRST CLASS LEVER

Force

Resistance

Fulcrum

BY SUSAN MCGRATH

110

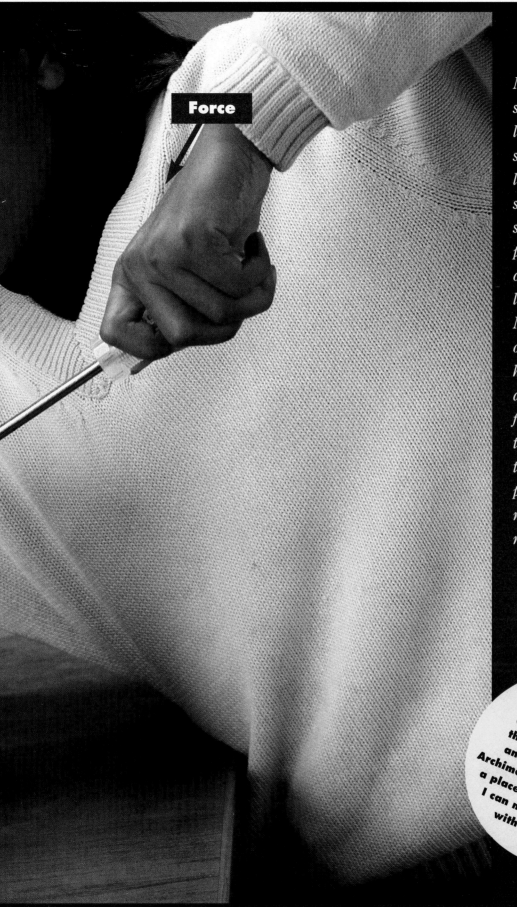

Force

Marissa uses a screwdriver to get the lid off a paint can. The screwdriver becomes a lever. The lever is a stiff bar (the screwdriver) that pivots on a fixed point, called the fulcrum (the lip of the paint can). Marissa pushes down on the screwdriver handle. The screwdriver turns on the fulcrum and the tip of the screwdriver pops the lid up. The lid, the part that is being moved, provides resistance.

Levers can move anything — in fact, the famous scientist and mathematician Archimedes said "Give me a place to stand on and I can move the Earth with a lever."

When you use a nutcracker,
you are using a different
kind of lever.
The fulcrum is at the end
of the lever.

You apply force
at the other end.
The resistance — a walnut —
lies between the force
and the fulcrum.
Squeeze, and the lever turns
at the fulcrum and crushes the nut.
You push down with a force,
and farther down the lever,
the force gets stronger.
A wheelbarrow works like
this, too! The wheel is
the fulcrum, the
force is your hands,
and the resistance is
the load of dirt in between.

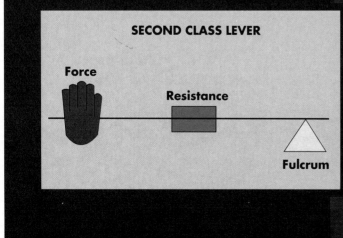

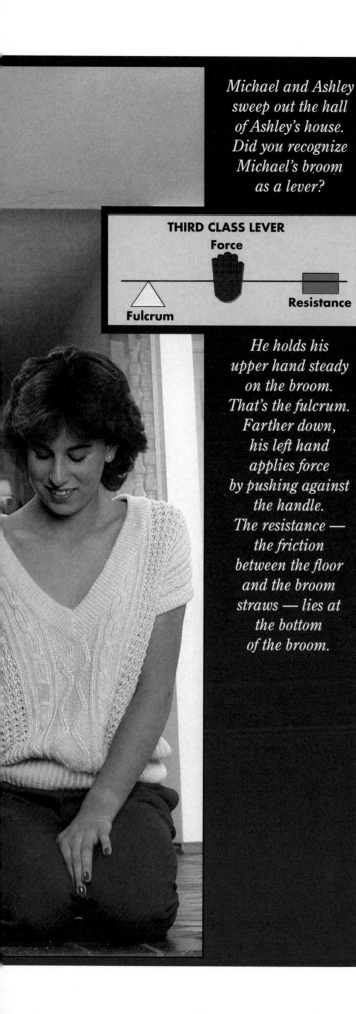

Michael and Ashley sweep out the hall of Ashley's house. Did you recognize Michael's broom as a lever?

THIRD CLASS LEVER

Force

Resistance

Fulcrum

He holds his upper hand steady on the broom. That's the fulcrum. Farther down, his left hand applies force by pushing against the handle. The resistance — the friction between the floor and the broom straws — lies at the bottom of the broom.

Try

THIS

Take a ball and throw it into the air. Hit it with your hand as if you were playing tennis. Note how far it goes. Try again, but use a racket or bat this time. What did you discover?

CHECK IT
OUT!

Your boxes are packed and you are ready to move to your new house. It's easy for you — the movers are going to take your stuff. That must be hard work. Talk to movers or people who deliver furniture to find out what simple machines they use to make moving and lifting easier.

113

BATTER UP!

Baseball pitcher Dwight Gooden is on the mound. The batter is in the box. Gripping the ball, Gooden winds up. He draws the whole right side of his body back. He keeps his left foot forward and his right foot back. Suddenly, he throws his weight forward. He whips his arm toward home plate and releases the ball. His arm works as a lever and magnifies the speed of the ball. The ball leaves his hand traveling about 145 km/h. It reaches the batter in less than half a second.

Imagine Gooden pitching that ball with his throwing arm tied to his side. The ball probably would, at best, roll slowly toward home plate. A pitcher's arm — and yours — is an effective lever. It lets you increase speed in many types of sports. In handball, your arm turns into a fast-swinging bat. In swimming, each arm is like a long paddle in the water. In hockey and in baseball, you hold long pieces of equipment that act as extensions of your arms. These extra-long levers hurl pucks or bats at fantastic speeds. And in tennis, your serving arm is the lever that aces your opponent!

Resistance

Force

Gooden uses his arm as a lever. At this point in the pitch, his forearm turns at the shoulder, which is the fulcrum. The muscles of his arm supply the force, and the ball provides the resistance.

UP AND OVER

Back in 1947, when Ulick O'Connor was the pole-vaulting champion of Ireland, pole-vaulters used bamboo poles. Bamboo did not bend too well. It often snapped. When it curved, it did not straighten out again.

Pole-vaulters would hear it splinter as they flew through the air.

Today, pole-vaulters use fiberglass poles. After bending, a fiberglass pole returns to its original shape. That is because it is made of elastic material. If you use force to change the shape of an elastic object, the object

Fulcrum

Steffi Graf shows the serving style that has helped her win dozens of important tennis tournaments.

Graf's serving arm and her racket work together as a lever. Her shoulder acts as the fulcrum, where her straight arm pivots. The muscles of her upper arm deliver the force. The resistance occurs where the ball hits her racket.

returns to its normal shape when the force is removed. That's what happens with a rubber band. The elastic quality of a fiberglass pole gives the vaulter a big boost. The world record vault

with a bamboo pole was almost five metres. The fiberglass record is more than one metre higher than that.

115

More Simple Machines

**Take a look around you.
Almost everything that moves is one kind
of simple machine —
or two, or more, working together.**

The ramp is a simple machine. It helps make heavy things easier to lift. Imagine how hard it would be to lift this wheelchair up a set of stairs. The wheels on the chair are simple machines, too!

Can you see other ramps, gears, and pulleys around you?

CHECK IT OUT!

Simple machines come in handy at a construction site. Visit a construction site so that you can watch these machines at work. If you observe with a classmate, you can talk about how simple machines are really the most important part of the monster machines that amaze us all. (Remember to stay well back from the site!)

116

This salad spinner works with the help of gears — also simple machines. Inside, a large gear moves around a smaller one when you turn the spinner's handle. Gears are two wheels with teeth that connect together to create motion. And they all act so that one gear turns faster or slower than the other, or moves in a different direction.

A pulley is being used to raise this flag to the top of the pole. It's easier for you to pull down on a string than to climb to the top of the pole with a flag in your teeth. The pulley, another simple machine, does the work of going up for you. Pulleys help us lift very heavy things, too. It's definitely easier to move a grand piano into a third-floor apartment by pulling down on a cable than it is to carry it all the way up.

PLAYING WITH SCIENCE

Simple machines are part of the fun in the new playground being planned at the Saskatchewan Science Centre. This model shows the science twists on some

schoolyard favorites. Notice the swings. Each has a different pendulum length. Which one would you like to push? Which one would you choose if you were pumping yourself? Now look at the giant levers. You will notice that the fulcrum is in a different place in each one. Which one would you use to lift your friend? Which would you use to lift three friends?

The wheelbarrow appeared in China 1000 years before it was known in Europe. It was used to move everything from pears to pigs to people!

HIGH TECH *On*

BY BOB MCDONALD

Don't be fooled by the simplicity of bicycle design. Even these old-fashioned bikes were high-tech for their time, and today's bikes are even more so. Their operation is pure science — in motion.

Wheels

Bullet-proof tires The first bicycles had no pedals and were made entirely of wood — including the wheels and tires! They were a kind of toy for grown-ups to sit on and push around. Today's bikes, of course, all come equipped with pedals. And most have strong, steel frames and rubber tires. The exceptions are the ultralight racing machines. They are made from the same lightweight carbon fiber plastics that were created for use in space. And some racing tires are made with silk and a material used in bullet-proof vests!

Today's cyclists on the move

Air lines

How you sit on your bike affects how you battle the force of the wind. On some bikes you sit upright, which is good for comfort. But if you want speed, you have to lower both the handlebars and your shoulders. This makes your chest and shoulders a smaller target area for the wind so it can't push against you as hard. Racers not only crouch low on their bikes, they also wear smooth, tight-fitting suits and helmets with a tail so that the air will slide smoothly over their bodies. Some racing bikes can also have enclosed wheels and frames. They help the bike resist the air even more — and they add that extra bit of speed that just might be enough to win a race.

Rollers — fat or thin?

Fat tires spread out your weight over a large area. That's why you can ride a mountain bike over sand without sinking in. But as fat, squishy tires roll along, they come in contact with a wide strip of ground, which slows them down. It's called rolling resistance. Racing tires, on the other hand, are thin and hard, so their contact area with the ground is as small as possible and the rider has very little resistance to overcome.

When a car is driven at high speed with the windows open, air rushes into the car. That means the engine has to work harder to stay at the same speed. With the windows closed, the shape of the car causes air to move around it easily. The car uses less fuel to stay at the same speed.

Gears — up or down?

Gears on your bike let you change how fast you pedal while your wheels stay at their speed. What's so great about that? In low gear, your legs move fast compared to your wheels. This gives you lots of power strokes in a short distance to help you climb hills or drive through soft sand.

RELAXING RIDES

Here's a glimpse of the recumbent bikes of the future! But don't toss out your old bike yet. It will be a while before this comfy exerciser will be seen all over city streets. This stretched-out bike was invented in the 1940s, but was

quickly banned from cycling competitions. The bikes of the day couldn't keep up with it. That's because this bike, and its laid-back rider, met with less air resistance than an upright rider on even the fastest racer.

Today's high-tech models are designed to reduce air drag, increase speed, and sometimes even hold more than one person!

High gear gives you many spins of the wheel for only a few strokes of your legs. That way, you can speed along downhill or along hard, level surfaces almost without trying. Without gears on your bike, you would have to pedal at the same speed as your wheels — dangerously slow going uphill and furiously fast flying downhill.

Whee

Great skate! Here come the bladers, whizzing toward you on wheels so hot they're cool. The wheels are on in-line roller skates. They give Jim and Kelly enough roller power to streak through a slalom course, high-stepping as they go. Kelly teaches at skating clinics, and both boys skate on a stunt team sponsored by a company that makes in-lines.

Jim and Kelly test a slalom course on in-lines.

24

BLADING BASICS

Cover up to avoid scrapes and other injuries. Wear elbow and knee pads, plastic wrist guards, safety gloves, and a helmet.

Learn how to stop before you get rolling. With your arms in front for balance, slide one foot forward and press hard on the brake pad under that heel.

Start off in a slight crouch. Put your weight on one foot and push off with the other, to the side and backward. If you feel unsteady, crouch a bit lower. Avoid skating too fast.

Learn on a smooth, flat surface. Always steer clear of traffic, people on foot, and obstacles.

With wheels lined up in a single row, in-lines differ from quads, the traditional four-wheeled roller skates. Ice-hockey players who wanted to practice off the ice began skating on in-lines, or blading, at the beginning of the 1980s. Since then, all kinds of people have learned they can have fun and get a good workout on in-lines. Jim says it's easier to move around on blades than on regular roller skates.

Most kids who blade say they learned the sport quickly. Balance is the main thing. Knowing how to roller-skate or ice-skate helps. The hardest part is learning how to stop.

As stunt team members, Jim and Kelly practice blading often. They make up new moves and perform at stores and sports events. They also blade with friends just for fun.

Says Kelly, "I wish I could stay on my skates all the time!"

Layne and Jim whirl in a double spin. Layne likes to freestyle, or do tricks, when she blades.

Above: A skater visiting a blading show in Los Angeles, California, tries out a pair of in-lines. Their new design is really old. More than 200 years ago, a Dutch inventor attached wooden spools in a row to his shoes, then "ice-skated" on pavement.

CHECK IT OUT!

Have you ever heard someone say that somebody else is trying to "reinvent the wheel"? People say the wheel is the greatest invention of all time. Brainstorm a list of things that use wheels. Try to find out the first use of the wheel. What is the strangest thing a wheel was ever used for? And what do you think the term "reinventing the wheel" means?

Speaking Of Plastic

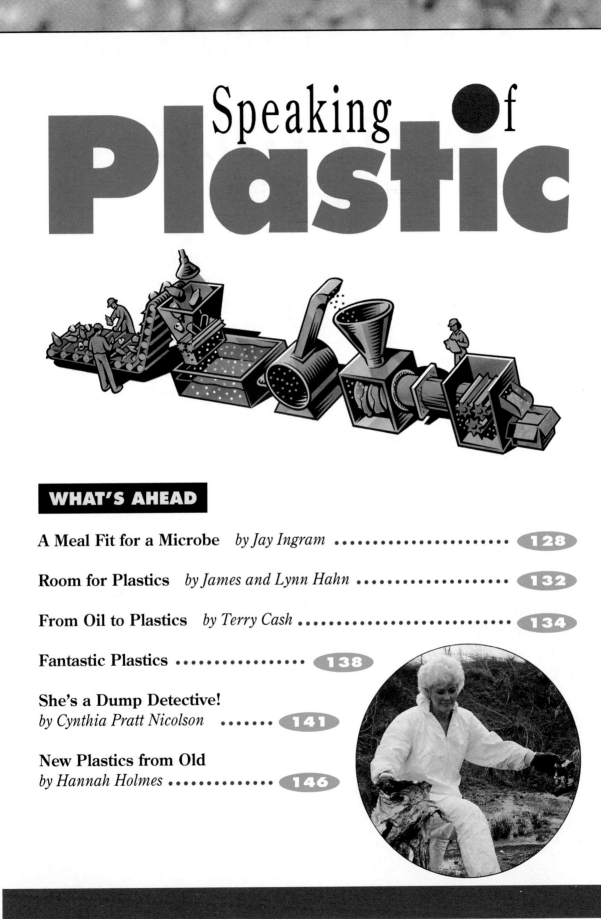

WHAT'S AHEAD

127

A Meal Fit for a Microbe

BY JAY INGRAM

Plastic is wonderful stuff:
it doesn't rust, it doesn't spoil,
and it doesn't fall apart
if you leave it outside all winter.

Plastic is terrible stuff:
it doesn't rust, it doesn't spoil,
and it doesn't fall apart
if you leave it outside all winter.

Yes, you read those two sentences correctly: plastics are good — and bad — for exactly the same reasons. They have lots of uses and they have changed everything from sports equipment to food wrapping. But they're bad because they don't go away. And plastics don't go away because nothing can eat them.

That's a bigger problem than you might think. Just about everything you see around you can be eaten by something or someone. If you forget about that orange in the corner of your knapsack, molds will pounce on it and turn it lovely shades of brown, green, and white. Leave a sweater in a cupboard long enough, and moths (actually their caterpillars) will chew enough holes in it to make it look like a piece of woolly Swiss cheese. Termites could chomp through most of your house if you let them. Believe

it or not, there are even microscopic yeasts (relatives of the ones that make bread rise) that live in your house and dine on the little flakes of skin that fly off your body whenever you move. But nothing exotic like this ever happens to plastic. It just piles up. That's because plastics aren't natural. We invented them. Most of the common ones today are no more than 30 or 40 years old. Before that, these materials had never existed on Earth. Thirty or 40 years isn't nearly enough time for nature to have come up with any kind of microbe that might like to make a meal out of a plastic cup. Given enough time, there will be microbes like that, but it may take hundreds, or even thousands, of years. For now, microbes just aren't prepared for plastics.

What can we do? We're using more and more plastic every year, and throwing out more and more, too.

When there's a really big problem like this scientists sometimes start to dream. And they can come up with some pretty amazing schemes. Some researchers have gone so far around on the plastic problem that they have ended up coming at it backwards. Rather than searching for some microbe that might be able to destroy plastics, they are looking for microbes that make plastics. And they have found them.

There actually are bacteria that, when times are tough and food is short, take the unusual step of making plastics. If they're put on a diet they aren't used to, they make an even better plastic than usual. It's their way of storing food. We store food as fat, or sometimes as sugar, for our muscles to use in emergencies. Plants store starch, but these tiny bacteria make and store plastic. If you see them under the microscope, they look like pods with peas in them, except that the peas are really little plastic blobs.

If the bacteria get really desperate for something to eat, they just digest these blobs. That's what makes these creatures so interesting. If they found the same plastic in a landfill, they'd eat it there, too. Although this plastic is made by bacteria, and not in a huge, modern factory, it is perfectly good plastic. So why not make everything out of this bacterial plastic? That way, when we throw it away, we just make sure that the bacteria are already there in the garbage dump. They'll feast on the plastic and we won't have such a big garbage problem anymore.

Unfortunately, like lots of wild ideas that sound great at first, this is not going to be that easy. For one thing, bacteria are pretty small — you could line up 10 000 of them single file across your little fingernail. So even if every one were just stuffed with plastic, you'd barely have enough to make a plastic Donald Duck to put on the head of a pin. And even if you grow trillions of them in big vats, they

don't make plastic very fast. That makes it expensive. Bacteria are just like people ... when they're forced to eat something they don't really like, they do it very slowly.

But why not dream some more? Just because the "machinery" for making plastic is naturally found inside a bacterium, that doesn't mean it has to stay there.

In fact, scientists have already been able to take it out and put it into the cells of a plant in the lab. If that works, and there doesn't seem to be any really good reason why it shouldn't, then maybe the ability to make plastic could be given to real crop plants, like sugar beets, or even corn. Imagine standing in a field holding a glistening, golden cob of corn in your hand, tearing the husk off, peeling away the silk, and seeing row after row of yellow kernels, all filled with ... plastic? Now imagine looking up and seeing a whole field of corn, swaying in the wind ... all plastic!

It sounds really neat doesn't it? But you have to be very careful about dream solutions for problems — sometimes you can overlook answers that might be easier, and better. While some scientists worry about how we can get corn plants to make plastic, the rest of us should just sit down and figure out how we can stop using so much plastic. Remember, what we don't use, we don't have to make.

It's fun to dream about plastic corn, but we all really need to think carefully when we buy plastic things. Plastics can be "permanent garbage," or they can be colorful objects that we enjoy and reuse. It's your allowance — spend it wisely!

SAVED BY PLASTIC!

What do 45-million-year-old spruce cones and Big Bird's feathers have in common?

Well, they both break down and eventually fall apart. But now they can both be saved — by plastic. Spraying a chemical called parylene (PAIR-ih-leen) on them creates a layer of plastic so thin that you can't tell it's there — Big Bird's feathers still feel soft.

Scientists who have studied the coating think it can survive 10 000 to 100 000 years before it would lose half its strength. Also, parylene does not react with other chemicals, which makes it safe for all kinds of uses.

Parylene is used in museums to preserve important pieces like those spruce cones. And Big Bird's feathered costume can now be put in a washing machine, scrubbed with cleanser, and blown dry!

— Stephen Strauss

ROOM for PLASTICS

BY JAMES AND LYNN HAHN

We live in a world of plastics. Almost everywhere we look, plastics are working to make life easier and less expensive. Most homes have plastics in every room. In the kitchen, plastics serve as mixing bowls, storage containers, countertops, and cutting boards. In the bathroom, we find plastic toothbrushes, combs, tiles, and sponges. Plastics make up many parts of radios, stereos, and TVs in the living room; and plastic, or partly plastic, alarm clocks in bedrooms wake people each day.

We could fill many books with lists of plastic things used in homes. Plastics are found in other areas of our life, too. Engineers use plastics to build rocket nose cones. Architects use plastics to build homes, stores, and offices. Many of our clothes are made from plastic fibers.

Obviously, all of the things we have mentioned are not made of exactly the same material. The word plastics includes a very large group of people-made materials that can be molded easily into many different shapes. Chemists use materials found in the earth to make plastics. The way finished plastic products look and feel depends on what they are made of and how they are made.

Some plastics, such as dinnerware, football helmets, and clock cases, are hard. Others, including squeeze bottles, cushion foam, and some toys, are soft. Both hard and soft plastics can be made clear, like glass. Plastic bags are soft and clear, while eyeglasses are hard and clear. Both hard and soft plastics can be made to look like almost anything, including silver, gold, wood, marble, and leather.

Take another look around your room — is everything just what it looks like? Or is some of it clever plastic? How many kinds of plastic can you find?

Look at the room pictured here. What do you see that is made of plastic? What would life be like without these items? Is there one thing that you just can't imagine living without?

Find as many different kinds of plastic — hard, soft, clear, colored — as you can. And don't forget to look for partly plastic things, too. Imagine how your running shoes would look if you could take the plastic out!

133

From **OIL** *to* PLASTICS

BY TERRY CASH

What's black
and gooey and
slimy and part of
your knapsack?
No, it's not the lunch
you left in there all
year — it's oil.

Plastic granules

Most plastics
(and your knapsack is probably one kind)
are made from chemicals that come
from oil. Each kind of plastic is made
from different chemicals.
A chemical factory turns the oil into
plastic granules, like the
ones you see here. Most plastics have no
color of their own,
so colored dyes are added.

The plastic granules are delivered to factories that make products such as bottles or bags. There are lots of different ways of making plastic products but they all have one thing in common. Plastic granules are heated until they go soft and runny, like syrup. Next, the soft plastic is made into different shapes. When the plastic cools down, it sets and keeps its new shape.

Some plastics can be shaped only once, but others can change their shape if they are heated again.

How plastic bags are made

Plastic bags are made from plastic that has been heated and rolled into thin sheets by machines with big, heavy metal rollers. It's just like rolling out modeling clay or pastry with a rolling pin. Can you roll out a sheet of clay as thin as a plastic bag?

This man monitors the machine as the plastic tubing is blown up in a big bubble (at the back of the photo). The plastic is then run through rollers to make it flat.

We can now make plastics that are ten times harder than steel.

How plastic bottles are made

Plastic bottles are made inside molds like the one in the photograph. The mold is made in the outline of the outside of the bottle. Bottle molds are often made in two halves, so the mold can be opened up to take out the bottle.

If soft plastic is blown up in the mold and then allowed to cool, it takes on the shape of the mold. This is called blow molding.

You can see how this works if you blow up a balloon inside a flower pot. As the balloon swells, it takes on the shape of the pot. It fits the sides so closely that you can lift the pot just by holding the end of the balloon.

Top: Bottle mold

Left: How the bottle mold works

How plastic buckets are made

Plastic buckets are made by squeezing, or injecting, the soft plastic into a mold through a narrow tube. This is called injection molding.

In the drawings, you can see how an injection molding machine looks inside.

First, plastic granules are fed into the machine through a big funnel. Inside the machine, the granules are heated until they melt. The liquid plastic is pushed, or injected, into the mold.

136

Ice-cold water around the mold cools the plastic so it sets in the shape of a bucket. When the plastic is cool, the mold opens and the bucket falls out of the machine.

When it comes out, the bucket has a stalk called a sprue, joined to the bottom. This is the plastic that was left in the narrow tube which squirted the plastic into the mold. The sprues are cut off — they can be reused.

Just imagine — all these products start off as an ooey, gooey mess. There's something to think about next time you get in trouble for having a messy room!

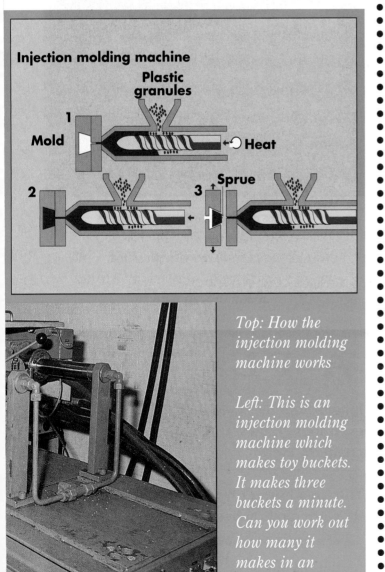

Injection molding machine

Top: How the injection molding machine works

Left: This is an injection molding machine which makes toy buckets. It makes three buckets a minute. Can you work out how many it makes in an hour?

Try

THIS

You can make your own mold out of clay — and then you can use it to have fun and create interesting gifts for your friends and family.

Press modeling clay on to a piece of tree bark or another interesting shape and carefully peel it off again. You will find the pattern of the bark in the clay. This is like a mold. Now mix up some plaster of Paris with water and pour it into your mold. When the plaster of Paris is hard, remove it from the mold. It will look like the tree bark pattern. What other molds can you make?

Note: Be sure not to pour the leftover plaster down the sink when you clean up. It will clog the drain. Also, wash your stirrer as soon as possible, or it will be covered with plaster forever.

— Terry Cash

CHECK IT OUT!

Oil is used to make fuel for your car, detergent, and perfume. Talk to a chemistry buff to find out what other things are made from oil.

FLASHBACK

A Sticky Situation

Sometimes mistakes are just mistakes. But a too-strong glue made by a lab technician in the mid-1950s created an exciting new use for plastic.

The lab technician worked at Tennessee Eastman in the United States. She was experimenting with different ways to stick thin pieces of glass used for cameras, or optical prisms, together. And what she made worked really well — too well.

When she tried to pull the very expensive prisms apart, they broke. And when she and her boss used the new glue on pieces of steel, they cracked the steel trying to pull it apart!

The glue was called Eastman's 910 Adhesive and it was one of the first super-glues. Look at this picture. The link you see was really two pieces glued together with 910 Adhesive. The link was attached to a crane used to lift — and hold — a car and the people in it!

SHE'S A DUMP

DETECTIVE!

BY CYNTHIA PRATT NICOLSON

Science experiments
don't always happen
in superclean, high-tech labs.
In fact, when Donna Police
wanted to investigate
different kinds
of plastic,
she headed for
one of the
dirtiest,
smelliest
places
you can
imagine —
a garbage
dump!

"How will I set things up?"

With the test strips ready, Police chose five different places to put them. One batch was left outdoors where the strips would be exposed to sun, wind, rain, and snow. Another batch was placed under fluorescent light indoors. Two batches were placed in cardboard boxes, and one box was lined with black plastic to keep out light. The two cardboard boxes were kept in a warehouse. With her last batch of plastic test strips, Police headed out.

At the landfill site, Police hired a bulldozer to dig a trench about three metres deep. She laid the wood slats at an angle in the trench and then had the bulldozer cover them over with soil and old garbage. Now it was time to wait.

"What changes do I see?"

After one month, Police went back to the dump and dug up her first sample. She also collected samples from each of her other test sites. These first test strips were removed from the wood slats, photographed, and checked for changes in color and appearance.

Police also used special machines to test the plastic strips. One machine measured the strength and stretchiness of each strip by slowly pulling it until it broke. Another machine was used to measure thickness. The results of these tests were carefully recorded for each strip.

For two years, Police and her helpers went back every month and collected samples from the five different sites. And every month they tested their samples and recorded the results.

Above: Test strips stapled to slats of wood

Right: You can see that after nine years, these plastic shoes are almost as good as new!

NO SANDWICH FOR ME, THANKS!

"It was a real eye-opener!" says Donna Police of her experiences digging into a landfill site. One astounding find was a loaf of bread that looked almost good enough to eat.

"It was incredible," says Police. "It looked as fresh as the day it was thrown away — there wasn't even a speck of mold on it!" Amazingly, that loaf of bread had been buried for over nine years.

How did Police know when the bread was buried? "We found dated newspapers, a calendar, and an old diary at the same level," she says.

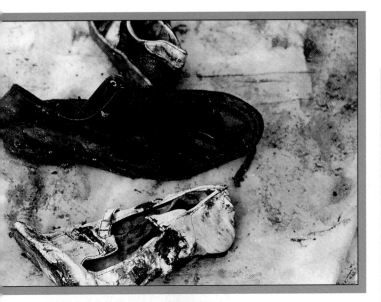

Look for these symbols on the bottom of most plastic bags and containers. The symbol tells the recycler what type of plastic it is, and helps in recycling.

"What have I learned?" At the end of her experiment, Police found that degradable plastics broke apart when they were left out in the sun and rain, but changed very, very slowly in the other conditions. Even after being buried in the mucky landfill site, most of the plastic strips came out just like new. "At first, I thought degradable plastic sounded like a good thing for the environment," says Police, "but now I've changed my mind." She worries that by adding things like cornstarch to make plastic degradable, we only make it impossible to recycle.

But what about all those people who want degradable plastic bags? Says Police, "We've decided to tell our customers to reduce, reuse, and recycle!"

New Plastics

Plastics. You know they don't go away. But the situation isn't awful. They can be reused — the plastics industry has always used its own scraps! And we now have the technology to recycle the plastic we use, such as pop bottles and yogurt containers.

1 Inspection

Workers inspect the plastic for rocks, glass, and plastics that the plant can't handle. Some plants can handle a mixture of plastics; others can't.

2 Chopping and Washing

Containers are chopped in a high-speed grinder and sprayed with water. Wash water is filtered and reused.

3 Floatation Tank

Mixed plastics are separated in a tank where some types sink and other types float.

FROM *Old*

BY HANNAH HOLMES

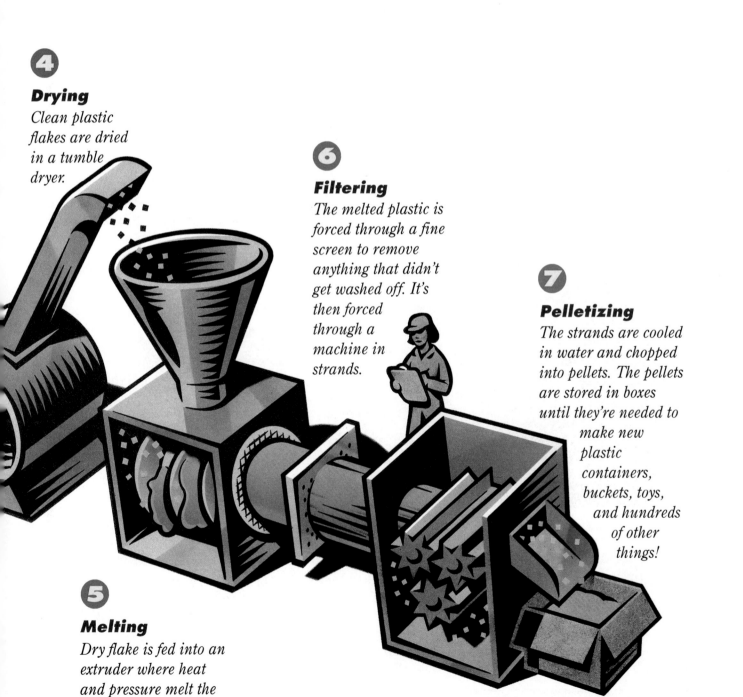

4

Drying
Clean plastic flakes are dried in a tumble dryer.

6

Filtering
The melted plastic is forced through a fine screen to remove anything that didn't get washed off. It's then forced through a machine in strands.

7

Pelletizing
The strands are cooled in water and chopped into pellets. The pellets are stored in boxes until they're needed to make new plastic containers, buckets, toys, and hundreds of other things!

5

Melting
Dry flake is fed into an extruder where heat and pressure melt the plastic.

147

TIMBER!

A company in Mississauga, Ontario, has found out how to turn used plastic into "lumber." This company makes "wood" out of the plastic containers that people throw away. The plastic is good for building outdoor things like park benches, picnic tables, road signs, and fence posts. The company will also make playground equipment and

seats for schools and other groups.

School kids are helping, too. Many of them collect juice boxes for the plastic "lumber" company to recycle.

This company is finding ways to turn a tough problem — what to do with plastic — into tough plastic lumber.

— Deborah Churchman

A plastic beverage container thrown by the side of the road will have a longer life than the person who threw it there.

CHECK IT OUT!

Plastics aren't used only to make other plastics. They're also used to make clothes. Fibers like nylon and acrylic are made from plastic. Find a good fabric store and spend some time reading labels. Think about how you would use the different materials for clothes, costumes, curtains, tablecloths, tents, or parachutes. Ask questions. Usually the people who work in fabric stores know a lot about the way different fabrics behave.

ROCK*on!*

WHAT'S AHEAD

Rocks and gems aren't the same thing — rocks are made up of two or more minerals, but a gem is made up of only one mineral.

SKiPPING STONES

BY JAY INGRAM

You don't have to be a scientist to know
what makes a good stone for skipping.
Most kids know it should be flat —
preferably on both sides — smooth,
rounded at the edges, and not too heavy.
The best stones fit nicely into your hand,
so you can curl your first finger
around them.

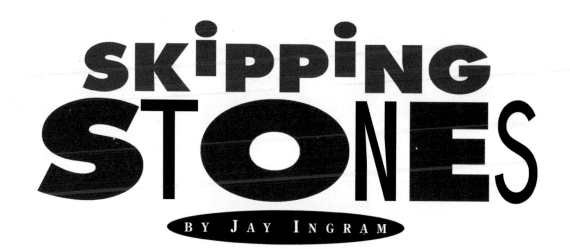

nd you don't have to be a scientist to know how to throw a skipping stone either. Most kids know you crouch down, and put a good spin on your throw.

But if you want to know exactly what happens when a stone skips, then it helps if you study skipping stones the way a scientist would.

A stone skips too fast for you to see exactly what it did. That's where high-speed photography comes in. You know how sometimes a photo catches you with a really silly look on your face?

That's because the camera stopped everything for that split-second. Normally, people would never see your face like that because it's always changing, from smiles, to frowns, to laughter. Scientists use high-speed cameras to take a photograph of an action that happens too fast for your eye to see.

If a stone is thrown the right way, the back edge hits the water first. The stone skids along the surface of the water like a surfer, and while it's skidding, it starts to stand up! Now it looks like a surfer, because a wave starts to grow under the front edge of the stone. An amazing thing happens then —

the stone lifts out of the water and flies through the air.

When it hits the water again, as long as the angle is right, it happens all over. (You can check *The Guinness Book of Records* to find out just how many skips are possible.)

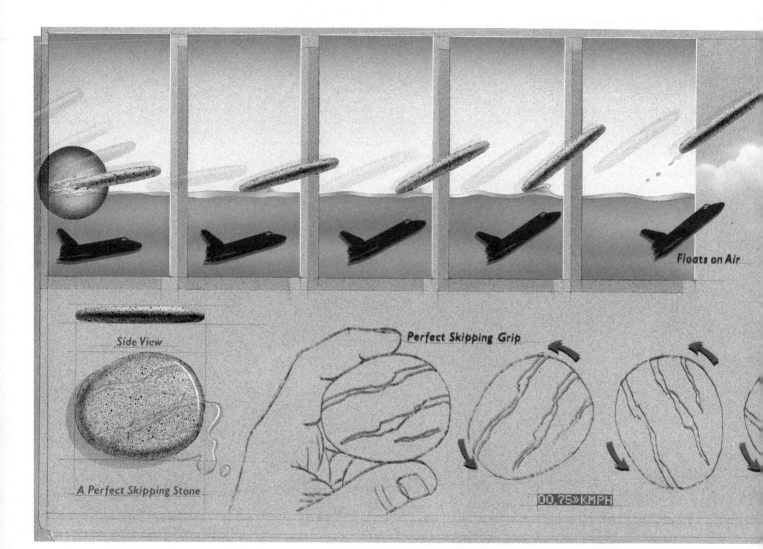

Floats on Air

Side View

A Perfect Skipping Stone

Perfect Skipping Grip

00.75»KMPH

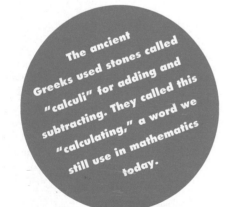

The ancient Greeks used stones called "calculi" for adding and subtracting. They called this "calculating," a word we still use in mathematics today.

What makes a good throw?

The stone has to spin just like a Frisbee™ or a top. That's what keeps it steady in the air. It should hit the water tail end first, but almost flat. And you should throw the stone pretty fast too — although speed really increases the distance between skips rather than the number of skips.

What makes the perfect stone?

The bigger the flat surface of the stone, the better it will skip, just like the bigger an airplane wing, the better it will fly. But the bigger the stone, the more it weighs and the harder it is to throw.

Hi-Tech Skipping Stone
Like Hollow Aircraft Wing

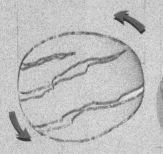

More Speed = More Distance

Skipping Stones

The perfect skipping stone would be hollow so it could have a large surface and still be light. And it would be waxed to give it a slippery surface. That way it wouldn't rub as much against the water every time it hit, which slows the stone down.

But if you did find the perfect skipping stone, and tested it, chances are it would be sinking into some lake or pond by the time you realized what you had just thrown away!

Try

THIS

Throw a Frisbee™ in the schoolyard. Try to bounce it off the ground to see how a skipping stone moves off the water.

Try making perfect skipping stones from clay. Predict what would be the best shape, size, and weight for a world-record skipping stone. You might even try making some hollow ones. Try them out in a nearby pond or lake.

CHECK IT OUT!

Does your idea of a good skipping stone have anything to do with the size of your hand or the way you throw? Compare your favorite stones with some of your friends' stones. Compare your hand sizes and throwing styles.

USEFUL
MINERALS

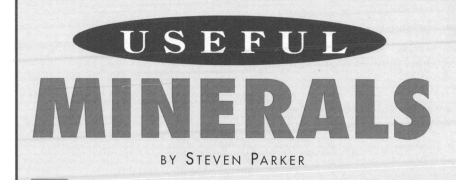

BY STEVEN PARKER

Everywhere you look you can see minerals. Some of them may have been taken from the Earth, cut, and polished into precious stones such as rubies or emeralds. Others do practical jobs. Diamonds, for example, aren't used only to make expensive jewelry. You'll also find them in many sorts of drill bits that are used to cut through rocks in mines or above oil wells. They are also used to make the needles on the record players that play old-fashioned vinyl records!

Diamond is the hardest natural substance on Earth, but it is made of carbon — the same material as the soft black soot in your chimney. Very few diamonds are good enough to be cut into gems for jewelry. The rest are used for a variety of jobs — usually cutting. Only a diamond can cut another diamond.

Gold has always been one of our most precious minerals. It is beautiful, easy to work with, and does not tarnish. Gold makes lovely jewelry, but it also makes fillings for teeth, electrical circuits, and solar cells for spacecraft.

Try
THIS

Use a microscope or a good-sized magnifying glass to look at pickling salt. Observe the size and shape of the crystals. How do they compare to those of table salt?

CHECK IT OUT!

What is the difference between 10K, 14K, 18K, and 24K gold? What is a carat? Find out from a jeweler or gemologist. Ask to see some samples!

Salt
is the crystal form of a mineral called halite. You can see the tiny cubes it forms if you look at a bit of table salt under a magnifying glass. Salt keeps food from spoiling. It also melts ice so it is sometimes spread on icy roads during winter.

Pyrite
is often mistaken for gold, so it is called fool's gold. Strike pyrite with a hammer and it sparks — it is sometimes used in lighters.

Corundum
is the hardest natural substance after diamond and is used to make beautiful ruby and sapphire jewelry, the bearings inside watches, and even emery for filing nails!

Quartz
is another common mineral in the Earth's crust. Amethyst (AM-uh-thist), rock crystal, and tiger's eye are all quartz. But quartz also shows up in electronic watches, sandpaper, and a variety of optical instruments.

Beryl
(BARE-ill) is usually green and one of its purest crystals is the emerald. You can find it in ordinary granite and the surrounding metamorphic rocks.

Sulfur
(also known as brimstone) easily catches fire and gives off strong fumes of hydrogen sulfide that smell like rotten eggs! The gunpowder for fireworks is made from sulfur.

FLASHBACK

Dorothy Crowfoot Hodgkin loved crystals. So this chemist spent her life studying them. You can find crystals in all sorts of things — from salt to copper to snowflakes. Scientists knew a lot about crystals before Hodgkin started her work, but Hodgkin was the person who discovered what crystals are like inside.

In high school, Hodgkin set up her own lab in her parents' attic where she grew crystals (she learned how to at school). She found out that no matter how crystals are formed, there are some ways that they are the same. They are all solid and have a regular shape. The pieces that make up a crystal fit together in a pattern that keeps repeating.

At Oxford University in England, Hodgkin learned about using X rays to see inside a crystal. The X ray would leave a picture of little dots that were the tiny pieces of the

Crystal Clear

crystal. She also worked on the math problems that helped her figure out how the crystal was put together.

Hodgkin and her research student Barbara Low made a big discovery in the late 1940s. They were given some crystals of the new drug called penicillin. The two women studied the crystals and, after much hard work, were finally able to see how the pieces of the crystal were made. That meant that the crystals and the drug could be made in large amounts to help sick people all over the world. Hodgkin also discovered how the crystals of vitamin B_{12} were made. Chemists have been using Hodgkin's discoveries to make medicines to treat all kinds of sicknesses.

Hodgkin won the Nobel Prize for Chemistry in 1964 for her important work with crystals and X rays — her work changed the face of modern medicine.

IT SHAKES
IT ROARS
IT THROWS
MELTED ROCK
INTO THE SKY
IT'S A

VOLC

BY CAROLINE WAKEMAN EVANS

ANO

It's 5:00 A.M. and I'm already wide awake. I live on a volcano — and when my windows start to rattle, I know it's time to get up.

I can see a friend of mine, Tina, standing on cool, hard lava at the edge of the lava river. She's holding a long metal rod that looks like a fishing rod. She dips it into the hot, flowing lava to take the lava's temperature.

I hold my breath as I remember a close call that Tina had recently. She thought she was standing on a bank of solid lava. Suddenly it cracked and started to split apart. As Tina leaped away, the place where she had been standing melted into the super-hot lava river. If she hadn't moved quickly, she could have fallen in and been badly burned or even killed. Today, though, she takes the river's temperature and calmly walks away.

The scientists also estimate the lava river's depth, width, and speed. They radio their findings back to the lab on top of Kilauea. On the helicopter radio I hear a scientist at the lab call them back. The measurements mean that this lava river might cause big trouble. It might flow over houses farther down the mountain.

Living with lava

The pilot circles the helicopter around the fountain one more time, and then we fly down the mountain. The lava river is flowing slowly and seems a long way from houses and the highway. Still, I'm sure that people who live in its path are being warned now of the danger. Some of the kids will be out of school helping their parents move to a safer place. These kids know that they might have to live with relatives for a while, but they love the island that volcanoes have created, and they love to see Kilauea's beautiful eruptions.

The pilot heads the helicopter back to the top of the volcano, and we land smoothly near the visitors' center. I can see the parking lot is already filled with cars. People, curious about what Kilauea's been up to, are waiting for my report. So I quickly take off my flight helmet and head over to them. I have a lot to tell them about that fountain of fiery lava.

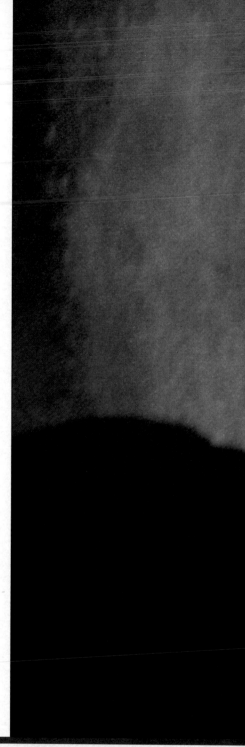

INSIDE KILAUEA

Kilauea is a broad and gently sloping volcano. It usually erupts quietly from a crater at the top (A), or from openings on its sides (B).

The drawing shows an inside view of the volcano. Deep inside Kilauea is a giant pool of super-hot melted rock, or magma (C). The melted rock has to squeeze through cracks inside the mountain, and that

causes small earthquakes. That's why the volcano shakes when magma is rising to the surface. If melted rock is thrown out of the mountain, the volcano roars.

The melted rock, now called lava, flows down the mountain and buries everything in its path. But as it cools and hardens, the lava becomes new land for the island of Hawaii.

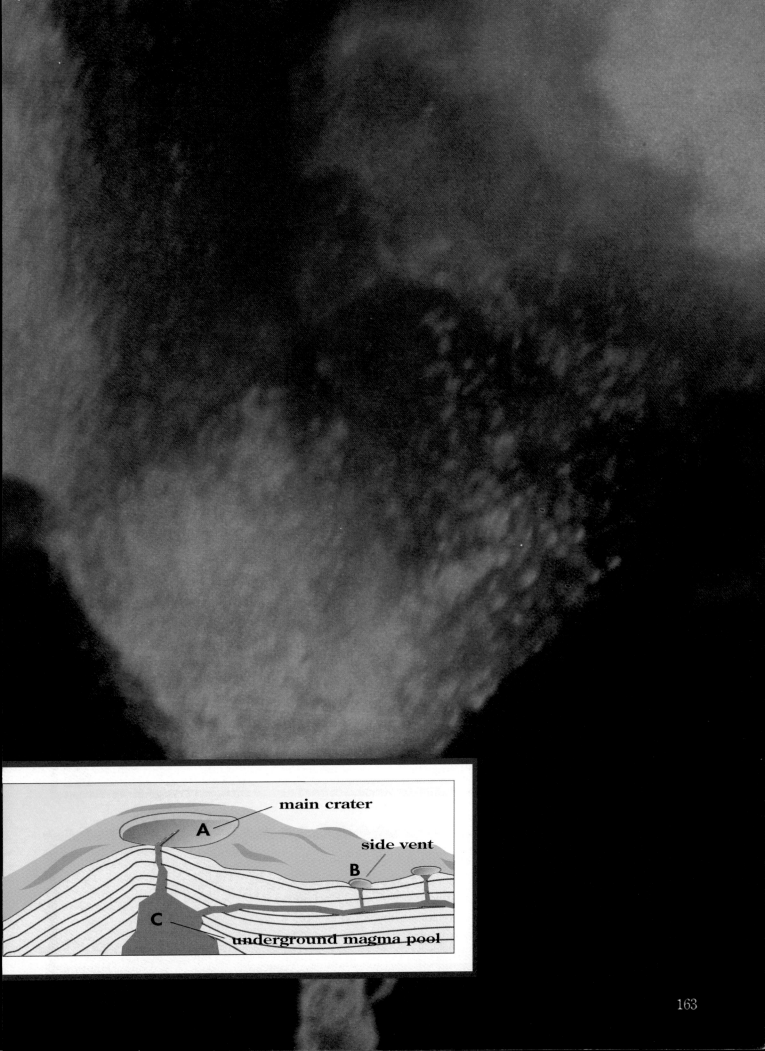

main crater

A

side vent

B

C

underground magma pool

FLASH**BACK**

Go for a dip in this colorful, football-field sized pool and you'll be swimming in part of an ancient volcano. In fact, anywhere you go in Wyoming's Yellowstone National Park, you'll be walking on the remains of a fire that's 600 000 years old.

The park's 200 fountains of water and steam are the result of three awesome eruptions. The last one was 600 000 years ago.

Volcanic Recreation

It was so powerful that it blew apart the crater from the eruption before it.

The area was visited in 1806 by a member of the Lewis and Clark exploration team. Seventy years later, another team of explorers spent time in the park naming many of the incredible features. They even named "Old Faithful," the famous geyser (GUY-zer) that erupts every 66 minutes.

CHECK IT OUT!

Many volcanoes are still active. Find out from newspapers or magazines where the most recent eruptions have been. Find out about Mount St. Helens, the volcano that erupted in Washington state in May, 1980.

Volcanoes are named after the Roman god of fire, Vulcan. People who study volcanoes are called vulcanologists — that's vul-CAN-o-lo-jists!

FOSSIL

HUNTING TIPS

FROM THE

EXPERTS

Read on to find out when
and where the experts go fossil-hunting
and how they bring their finds
back to the museum.
You can use some of their tips
to find your own fossils.

BY KATHERINE GRIER

Where to look

Fossils are usually found in one kind of rock, called sedimentary rock.

Sedimentary rock forms when bits of soil or seashell settle onto the Earth or sea bottom. Layers of these sediments build up and, after a very long time, turn to stone.

So if you go fossil-hunting, look for flat layers of sedimentary rock. You are likely to find them along the shores of lakes and rivers, along roads cut through rock, or in quarries where stone or gravel has been taken from the ground.

Sedimentary rock shows up in all sorts of landscapes. How come? Tremendous forces within the Earth are always slowly moving the rocks of the Earth's crust. For instance, the Burgess Shale is one of the best places in Canada for exceptional fossils. It was once a seabed. Now it lies high on the slopes of the Rocky Mountains.

When to look

Spring is a good time to hunt for fossils. Winter rains, winds, and snow have scrubbed the rocks and worn away their softest parts. Fossils that were hidden are now exposed.

FOSSIL HUNT SAFETY AND MANNERS

- Sometimes you'll find an exciting bed of sedimentary rock on private property. Be sure to get permission to collect. If you're in a national park, pay attention to the rules — do not remove any fossils from the park.

- If you do go to a quarry, stick to the quarry floor where there's no danger from falling rock.

- Watch out for flying rock chips whenever you're using a hammer or chisel. Wear safety glasses and sturdy gloves.

How to look

If you find a thick slab of rock, look at its sides to see if it's in layers. If it is, you may be able to use a hammer and chisel to split it open. Turn the slab on its side, fit your chisel along the edge of a layer, and give it a good whack with your hammer. You never know what you'll find inside.

Above: Giant toad fossil
Top left: Sedimentary rock
Bottom left: Dragonfly fossil

If you find a fossil in dark-colored rock, breathe on it or wet it. The water or the moisture in your breath will darken it and help you see what's there.

If you find a fossil in super-hard rock, use an old toothbrush to loosen dry dirt or to scrub it under running water. A little dishwashing soap in water will finish the cleaning job when you get home.

Be sure to test your cleaning method (scrubbing under water, especially) on a corner or a piece that you don't mind losing.

Soft, moist, or crumbly rock needs special care to keep it from falling apart. Wrap it in a damp paper towel and put it in a plastic bag. When you get home, treat it to make it stronger. Or treat it on the spot. First, make a mixture of white glue and water (half and half). Next, brush the mixture over the rock, top and bottom — but not on the fossil itself. Let the mixture soak in and dry.

Keep your fossils from rubbing against one another in your pack. Wrap them in some paper towels or newspaper.

EGG TIMERS

Ostrich eggshells are all over ancient spots in the Middle East and Africa. Stone Age people ate the yolks and used the shells as canteens. Now scientists are experimenting with using the shells as clues to the past.

It seems that ostrich eggshells can be used to tell the age of fossils and other items that appeared on Earth between 10 000 and 200 000 years ago.

The shells are useful because they fall apart very slowly, and keep a certain level of amino acids (part of the protein that builds the shell). Archaeologists measure that level and figure out when the egg was laid. They can then find the age of nearby objects.

So eggs aren't just for breakfast anymore!

An Ancient
EGYPTIAN
MAP

BY JAMES A. HARRELL

In a small ancient house made of stone, mud, and thatch, an old man sat hunched over a bench. He was finishing a map he had been making. It was about half a metre wide and nearly three metres long, and it was drawn on papyrus.

Amennakhte's house

168

The old man's name was Amennakhte (a-mo-NOKD) and he was a scribe in the service of the High Priest of Amun. The time was 3150 years ago, and the place was the village of Deir el-Medina (DEAR-el-meh-DEE-na), near Thebes and the Nile River, in Egypt.

James Harrell in Egypt

My name is James Harrell and I am a geologist with an interest in archaeology. I study the rocks and minerals used by the ancient Egyptians. One day I was looking at a book about Egypt and I saw a picture of Amennakhte's map. The book said that the map had been found 170 years earlier in the ruins of Deir el-Medina.

It is a very famous map because it is the only one to survive from ancient Egypt. It is also the oldest known map in the world. There was, however, a great mystery surrounding it — no one knew for sure what area in Egypt it showed. No one knew who drew it, or when exactly it was made.

A ROCK HOUND'S
Dream

Pack your bags, your hiking boots, your journal, and a lot of energy. You're about to start on a worldwide adventure — the rock hound's dream vacation!

Volca

First stop, Ayers Rock. This huge sandstone outcrop is the largest rock on the Earth's surface. You're one of the thousands of tourists who come to central Australia's hot, dry Outback each year to see — and climb — the rock. This photograph was taken from someone's garden in a town nearby.

Let's stay in Australia but move to the west. No, you are not at the coast — you are over 300 km inland, at Wave Rock. The granite this rock is made of is about 270 million years old. It's part of the ancient rock that forms the base of Australia.

How about a stop in Ireland to see a giant rock highway? It juts into the sea and looks like it links Ireland to Scotland. This is the Giant's Causeway. It was really formed by lava pouring out from underneath the Earth's surface.

Now to southern Alberta, to Milk River in Writing-on-Stone Provincial Park. The valley was formed during the last ice age (10 000 years ago). Wind and water have worn away the soft sandstone to create this unreal scene.

A trip to the United States comes next. In southern Utah there are more than 200 natural sandstone arches like this one in Arches National Park. This is Delicate Arch, and it's 10 m wide.

Four hundred kilometres from the arches is Bryce Canyon. Take a good look at these craggy-topped limestone columns — they are called hoodoos.

Getting tired? Sit down, relax. This part of the tour is over. But your adventure with rocks has just begun. Where do you think you'll go next?

ALLENDE METEORITES

If you were a sixth-grader living in Pueblito de Allende, Mexico, in 1969, you wouldn't have had to travel very far to see some rocks that were really out of this world!

News of a huge meteorite, or a rock that falls from space, came at 1:00 a.m. on a winter's morning. The fragments from the rock were scattered in a broad path over the farmlands of the area. These meteorites were very exciting, for there were a lot of them. It was clear from the start that they were a rare type. Brian Mason and Roy Clarke, Jr., from the National Museum of Natural History in Washington, D.C., rushed to investigate.

Sixth-graders out looking for meteorites

The following day, an entire sixth grade was let out of class to help with the search. Their directions were to walk side by side in a line toward the foothills.

They were to yell when they saw a black rock that appeared to be unusual. There were six finds, from one the size of a grapefruit to a rock that weighed almost 10 kg.

Such meteorites had been found before, but they were very few and very small. Near Pueblito de Allende, so many meteorites were found that it was possible to share them with scientists around the world.

It is almost certain that the white bits inside the black rock — the calcium-aluminum inclusions — are even older than the black rock around them. The black rock itself is the usual older-than-Earth stuff. But the white bits are from time and space and stars beyond the solar system. They are most likely bits of interstellar dust from an exploding supernova, and can help reveal the origins of the solar system.

But not all meteorites are this exciting — or even real! The National Museum of Natural History has received lots of meteorites-that-are-not-meteorites. One "meteorite" appeared on a sidewalk during a storm. A light flashed, wrote the sender, and then he saw a rock that wasn't there before. How to tell him the gritty object must have slipped off a shoe in the rain, the "inclusions" in it were sand, and his meteorite was a hard wad of chewing gum?

— Peggy Thomson

THIS FOOD'S A ROCK-SOLID HIT

These desserts look tempting,
but Sarah won't taste them.
Eating them might bring on
dental disaster.
The pear and brownies,
caramel popcorn, yellow cake,
chocolate pie, and light and
dark fruitcakes are all as hard as rocks.
In fact, they are rocks.

ANCIENT FOOD

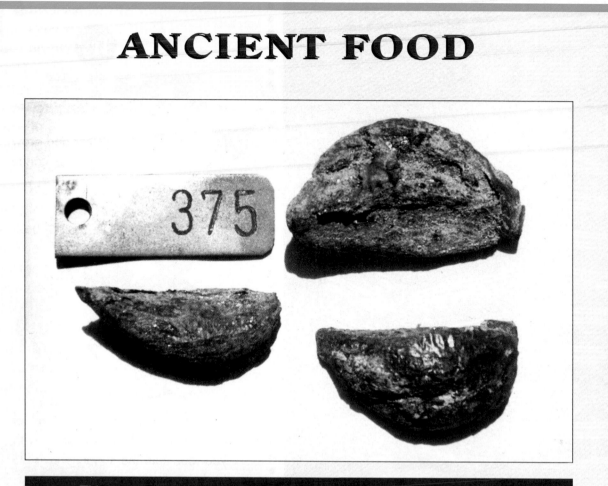

This 2000-year-old garlic looks almost the same as some you might see today!

In 79 A.D., the volcano Vesuvius erupted and covered the city of Pompeii, Italy, with ash.

Although the people are long gone, detailed remains of foods — made of ash that became rock hard — still exist. And archaeologists like Frederick Meyer, a scientist at the United States Department of Agriculture, are still uncovering clues about the ancient city.

Meyer is finding perfect remains of all kinds of foods — figs, olives, lentils, onions, and garlic. "Vesuvius created an incredible store of information about the history of agriculture," says Meyer. "This gives us a record of what the Romans were eating almost 2000 years ago."

— Elizabeth Keyishian

Photo courtesy of Fredrick G. Meyer, Supervisory Botanist, United States Department of Agriculture.

BUSY BODIES

WHAT'S AHEAD

BLINKING
PUZZLERS

BY JAY INGRAM

Every time you blink,
your eyes close,
but you never notice
that they do.
Yet if someone
turns the room
lights out —
even for
a shorter time
than a blink —
you see the room
turn black.

Why doesn't
it turn black
when you
blink?

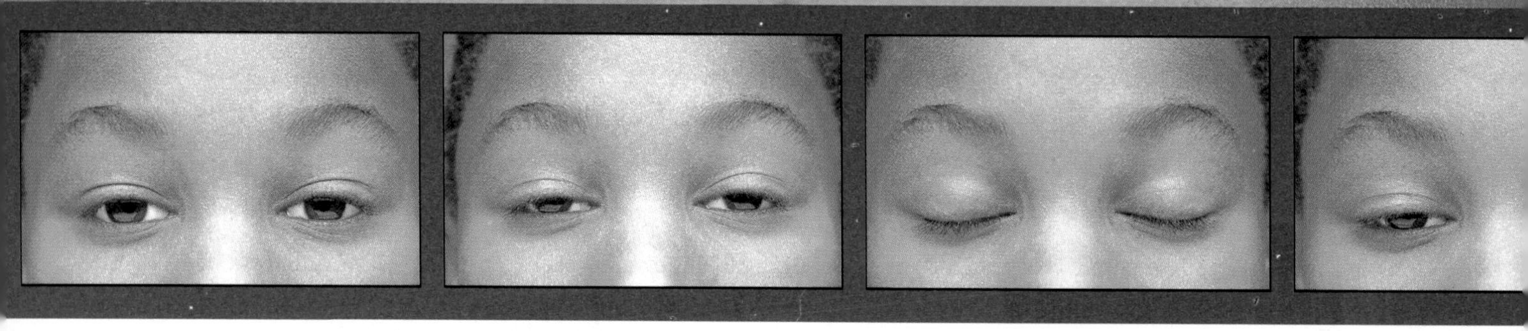

Scientists have discovered that just before you blink, a signal goes out from your brain to your eyes, telling them to shut off. As soon as the blink is finished, your eyes are turned on again. So your eyes never send the message, "Hey! It's dark in here!" because they're turned off. But your eyes are still on when the room lights go out, and they notice the darkening right away.

Our eyes need only two blinks every minute to stay moist, but we blink 15 times a minute. Do we need the extra 13 blinks?

No, we don't. This is the most surprising thing about blinking. The number of times you blink, and when you blink, are controlled by what you're thinking about and paying attention to. That sounds strange, but all kinds of experiments have shown it to be true. There's one rule for blinks: the harder you're concentrating, the less you blink. As you read this you've probably slowed your blinking from 15 a minute down to six or seven. But there's probably a blink coming up — right now — because you've reached the end of this line.

Normally, if you weren't paying attention to your blinking, you probably would have blinked right then because your mind had a chance to relax and stop reading. But now you're reading again, so you won't be blinking for a while. And you'll blink even less if you do this puzzle in your head:
17 - 5 + 10 + 4 = ?

Scientists aren't really sure why we blink less when our brains are working hard, and why we save our blinks for those moments when our brains can take a break. But they're pretty sure

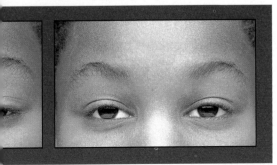

it's just accidental — you can't stop people from thinking by taping their eyelids shut!

Try to watch friends, family members, or pets without them knowing. Count how many times they blink in 30 seconds.

HINT Scientists often discover a lot simply by watching closely and keeping track of what they've noticed.

BLINKING FACTS

• We all blink about 15 000 times a day, and each blink takes less than half a second. That means that you spend about an hour and fifteen minutes of your waking time each day with your eyes partly or completely closed.

• When you blink, your eye is completely closed for only about one-twentieth of a second.

BEYOND BLINKING

Do you ever wonder why you shiver when you're cold, or why you long for a cold drink on a hot summer's day? Your brain "tells" your body to put on that thick coat to help you warm up or to have a glass of cold water to cool down.

Your brain sends messages to your body all the time — and you might not know that some of the things that you do without thinking, or automatically, are a result of these messages from the brain.

Why do people blush?

People blush for different reasons — they're scared, they're nervous, they're embarrassed. When you get scared, nervous, or embarrassed, you lose control of the blood vessels in your skin.

All of them open at once and the blood rushes to the surface — so you get all red and feel really warm! It happens automatically, so there's nothing you can do to stop a blush once it starts.

What is a hiccup?

Scientists aren't completely sure what causes a hiccup. Some believe that the problem is caused by the epiglottis (ep-ih-GLAW-tiss), which is a piece of flesh at the top of your voice box that flaps up and down. The epiglottis is designed to keep things such as water, saliva, and food from sliding down into your windpipe. It is supposed to move in rhythm with your breathing. Sometimes, though, the epiglottis gets out of rhythm. Some scientists think that this gives you hiccups.

— *OWL Magazine*

Try **THIS**

Talk to your classmates and family members to find out their best hiccup cures. Next time you get the hiccups, try a cure that you have never tried. Remember to share your cures the next time someone has the hiccups.

CHECK IT OUT!

If you think hiccups are funny, read *Hiccup Champion of the World*, a hilarious novel by Ken Roberts.

Only about two of every 10 people are left-handed.

OUR BEST S

Here is Vahirda. She is two months old. Today Vahirda is going to get the first vaccine (vak-SEEN) of her life. The vaccine will protect Vahirda from three diseases: diphtheria (dip-THEER-ya), whooping cough, and tetanus. In the next few months, and throughout her life, Vahirda will get many other vaccines. But what is a vaccine? And how does it protect us? Let's first look at what causes disease.

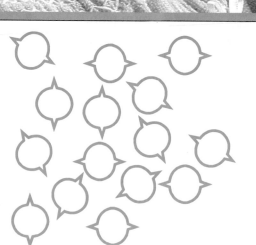 

Invading microbes

These invading microbes might cause disease. Our bodies send antibodies, shaped to lock around the microbes, to destroy them.

188

HOT

BY CAROLE BRODEUR

Disease is caused by pathogens. These can be viruses or microbes — tiny organisms which you need a microscope to see. Viruses and microbes are everywhere, in the air, water, and soil. Most microbes are harmless to humans. We even put some of them to work for us, to make food or medicine. But a few microbes or viruses can make us sick.

Viruses can invade cells in our body and turn these cells into virus-making factories. Bacteria are a kind of microbe. They can attack the cells in our body and use them for food, or they can poison the cells in our body. When the body is invaded, we get sick. Luckily, vaccines can protect us from many serious diseases.

Antibodies — the body's soldiers

When Vahirda got her vaccine, at two months, she was injected with tetanus, diphtheria, and whooping cough microbes. Vahirda didn't have anything to fear. They were treated so that they were too weak to cause disease. Still, Vahirda's body could become familiar with these microbes. The human body can recognize these invaders and make armies of soldiers to defend itself. The soldiers are called antibodies. Different antibodies are made to defend against each different type of invader.

Defending antibodies

NO MORE CHICKEN POX

Have you ever had chicken pox? Wouldn't it be great if there was something you could have done to make sure you never got it? Well, you may be out of luck, but kids in the future might not be. Doctors are working on a chicken pox vaccine for children. (There is one for adults. Chicken pox can make adults very ill.) The patent will soon be given to make this vaccine. The vaccine would be given to all children at the age of 15 months, so kids in the future might never have to fight those itchy spots!

Track star Wilma Rudolph was the first Black and the first American woman to win three gold medals in an Olympic games. She got over fights with double pneumonia, scarlet fever, and polio to become a championship runner!

FLASHBACK

Dr. Sara Josephine Baker

In the summer of 1902, 1500 babies died every week in New York City. It happened every summer, and there did not seem to be anything that could be done. When the hot weather came, babies just got sick, and many of them died.

But that summer, a young doctor started working for New York's Public Health Department. She was Dr. Sara Josephine Baker. Every day, Baker saw sick and dying babies and their helpless mothers. She knew that something had to be done.

For the next five years, Baker did all kinds of jobs for the health department. But she kept thinking about all those babies dying each summer.

At that time, the idea that microbes cause sickness was new even to doctors. Most people did not understand it at all. When the weather was hot, food and milk, left out in the open and uncovered, spoiled. Flies and insects were everywhere, carrying diseases. Baker thought that if she could teach mothers about hygiene (HI-jean), or the science of cleanliness and good health, fewer babies would get sick and fewer would die.

Finally, in 1908, Baker got the chance to test her idea. The health department gave her a job for the summer as the Director of the Bureau of Child Hygiene, a center to teach people about keeping children clean and healthy. If she could show that her ideas were helpful, she could have the job for good.

The groove between your nose and your upper lip is called the philtra.

CHECK IT OUT!

Edward Jenner first discovered microbes, and Louis Pasteur figured out how they could be used to help prevent diseases. Find out how these scientists made their discoveries.

How often do adults need booster shots? Talk to your parents or your doctor to find out.

Baker started in early summer with 30 nurses. She picked a part of the city where people were very poor and lived in crowded apartments. In the summer, it was terribly hot, sticky, and dirty.

At that time, most babies were born at home. Baker would get a list of the births from the day before. The nurses would then visit the mothers and tell them how to take care of the new babies. They would tell the mothers to nurse the babies instead of giving them bottles, which could be dirty or contain spoiled milk. They would tell the mothers to wash the babies often, to dress them in light summer clothes (or even in nothing but a diaper), and to take them out to the park for some fresh air every day.

By the end of the summer, as many babies as ever had died in the rest of the city. But in the section where Baker had worked, there were 1200 fewer deaths than in the summer before.

The health department was impressed, and the Bureau of Child Hygiene became a permanent institution.

— Sarah Flowers

What if Vahirda wasn't vaccinated?

If Vahirda had caught whooping cough, her body would still have created antibodies. But her body would have produced them much more slowly, because this would be its first meeting with the whooping cough microbe. The microbe would have had the time to multiply and to make Vahirda very sick.

One year later

Imagine that a year later Vahirda is exposed to the bacteria that cause whooping cough. Since she was vaccinated against whooping cough, her body will remember this invader and know how to make antibodies against it. These antibodies will stick to the invading bacteria. White blood cells will have the job of finding the antibody-coated invaders and destroying them. Antibodies will tell the white blood cells to eat the invaders and the enemy will be defeated!

The booster shot

Here is 13-year-old Martin. Martin has just had his vaccination against diphtheria, tetanus, and whooping cough. Like Vahirda, Martin also had a vaccination when he was two months old. Why repeat it?

Several years after getting a vaccine, the body begins to forget how to produce antibodies. The body's memory must be refreshed by another visit from the pathogens. Martin knows this. He gets vaccinated to guard against sickness.

ALERT

Mummy Gets a Checkup

No, this isn't a case of very slow ambulance service.

But the patient, a nearly 3000-year-old mummy,

is headed for the hospital.

A doctor in Boston, Massachusetts, offered to give

the ancient Egyptian a checkup using modern medical

technology. He hoped to take a new look at old history.

Let's see what he found ...

Myron Marx is a doctor who happens to be fascinated by mummies. Tabes (TAH-bess), an Egyptian woman who lived some 3000 years ago, is a mummy in the Museum of Fine Arts in Boston. Wouldn't it be interesting, Marx thought, to use modern X-ray techniques to examine the mummy without so much as opening the sealed case?

The museum agreed. Actually opening the case might damage the mummy. But a computerized X-ray machine called a CT scanner could explore it safely. With the scanner, Marx electronically strips away the case and hundreds of metres of linen wrapping.

On the way to the hospital

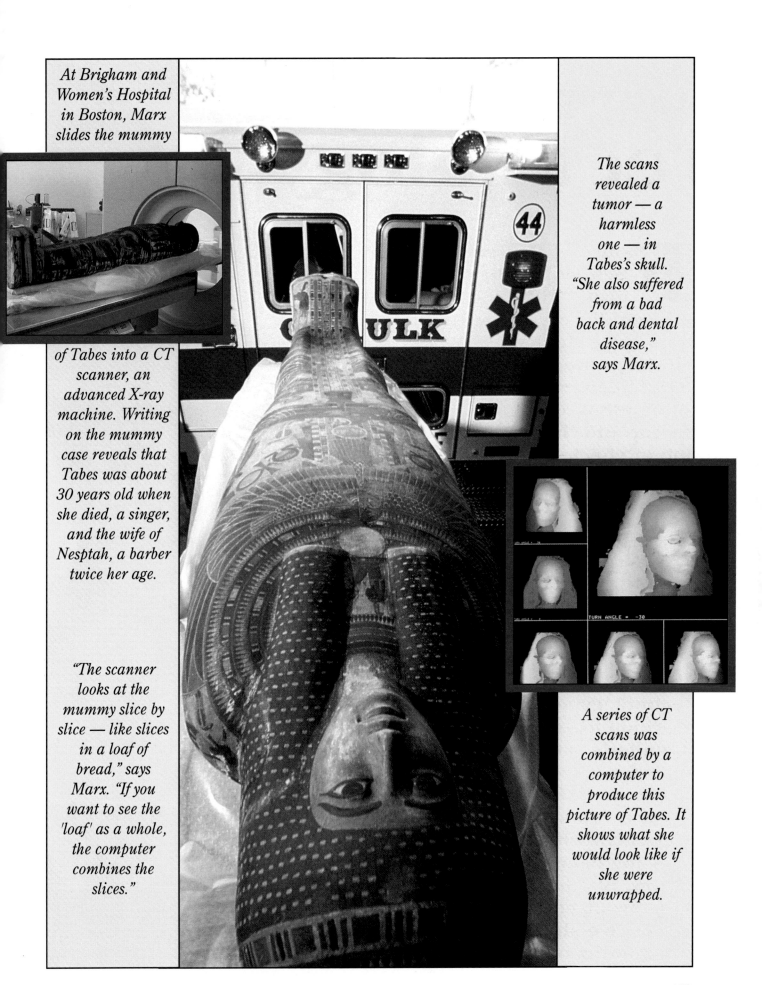

At Brigham and Women's Hospital in Boston, Marx slides the mummy of Tabes into a CT scanner, an advanced X-ray machine. Writing on the mummy case reveals that Tabes was about 30 years old when she died, a singer, and the wife of Nesptah, a barber twice her age.

"The scanner looks at the mummy slice by slice — like slices in a loaf of bread," says Marx. "If you want to see the 'loaf' as a whole, the computer combines the slices."

The scans revealed a tumor — a harmless one — in Tabes's skull. "She also suffered from a bad back and dental disease," says Marx.

A series of CT scans was combined by a computer to produce this picture of Tabes. It shows what she would look like if she were unwrapped.

Technology

BY MARGO BEGGS

Fourteen-year-old Jennifer Schoenhals has a bionic arm! "That doesn't mean she can lift cars, though," says Greg Bush. Greg works at the Hugh MacMillan Rehabilitation Centre in Toronto. It's his job to check Jennifer's arm to make sure it's working properly. Greg explains that "bionic" doesn't mean super-strong. It means that the body and technology are working together. Jennifer's arm is also called a myoelectric (my-o-ee-LEK-trik) arm. It replaces her right arm which is missing below the elbow. She has had her myoelectric arm since she was 18 months old.

Here, Jennifer and Greg talk about myoelectric limbs, such as arms and hands, and how they work.

Margo: How does the arm go on?

Jennifer: It grips my arm around the elbow and holds on by suction. When I want to take it off, I just give it a little tug.

Margo: Is it heavy?

Jennifer: You have to get used to it. The older you get, the bigger and heavier the arm gets. I get a new arm about every two years.

Margo: Besides getting bigger, does the arm change as you change?

Jennifer: Yes. It is designed to look very natural. For example, the arm is designed to show your veins as you age.

Margo: What other myoelectric limbs are there?

Jennifer: One of my friends has a myoelectric leg. I can't believe how real it looks.

Margo: Can you use your arm to play sports or do other activities?

Jennifer: No, I have to use different arms for different things. The hand I use in gym class is shaped like a scoop. With volleyball I was having trouble serving because the fingers wouldn't hold the ball. With this special arm, the ball fits into the scoop nicely. I also have a swimming arm. It's waterproof and shaped like a paddle.

CUTTING EDGE

ALL EARS!

Imagine an artificial, or prosthetic (pross-THET-ik), ear that could allow the hearing-impaired to hear! Scientists all over the world are working on one that can. The invention is called a cochlear (KOKE-lee-ar) implant — it replaces the tube, or cochlea, filled with the tiny hairs that change sound to electricity so the brain can read it. If the cochlea is destroyed, the hairs cannot vibrate and create those electric signals. This implant vibrates when a sound is made. The vibrations create an electrical impulse that is sent to the brain.

The tricky part is "translating" the sounds to electricity. Doctors have to find out what, say, "p" is in electricity. When doctors figure that out, they may have come up with whole new way to get the message!

Margo: Is there anything you can't do with a myoelectric arm?

Jennifer: I can't think of anything that could really stop me. I wasn't going to take horseback riding because I thought the arm would hold me back, but I went ahead and tried. It's really going well — I'm jumping now.

Greg: We work with people all the time to meet their special needs. One girl wanted to play polo, and Jennifer helped us find ways to help her out. We come up with something new every day.

Margo: What does the term myoelectric mean?

Greg: *Myo* is Greek for muscle. Myoelectric means a muscle is controlling an electrical device.

Margo: How does your myoelectric arm work?

Jennifer: I use the muscles in my arm to make the hand open and close.

Greg: There are small electrodes, about the size of a dime, built inside the arm. When Jennifer flexes her muscles, they give off a small electrical current. The electrodes, which are like little antennae, send the current to an electric switch in the arm. The switch turns on a small motor that makes the hand move.

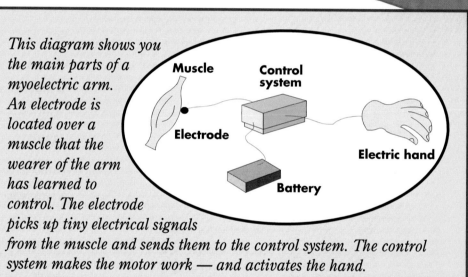

This diagram shows you the main parts of a myoelectric arm. An electrode is located over a muscle that the wearer of the arm has learned to control. The electrode picks up tiny electrical signals from the muscle and sends them to the control system. The control system makes the motor work — and activates the hand.

Muscle Control system Electrode Electric hand Battery

A HAPPY CAPTAIN HOOK

If Captain Hook were alive today, chances are he'd be called Captain Myoelectric. And he'd probably be a lot less grumpy! Myoelectric hands and arms have been designed to replace hooks. People like them better because they look so natural that others don't even notice them. Myoelectric hands can also grip much better than hooks. As well, they are much more comfortable to wear. Hooks must be held on by a harness. Myoelectric arms slip on as easily as a glove.

WATCH OUT, CROC!

Margo: Does the arm need special care?

Jennifer: Well, because I use it when I ride horseback, the glove that covers the hand gets dirty. So I have to get it replaced every time I come in. Also, the arm has batteries in it. These have to be recharged every night. I plug the arm into an electrical outlet from a plug on the side of the hand.

No two people have the same fingerprints — even identical twins have different ones!

It was in the 1950s in Germany that myoelectric limbs were first introduced. The first child anywhere in the world to get a myoelectric arm was in Canada, in 1965, at the same center where Jennifer Schoenhals goes today. The Hugh MacMillan Rehabilitation Centre is world famous for its work in myoelectric technology. Patients of all ages have come to the center from as far away as Australia, Ireland, and Mexico.

These players have learned to use flexibility, balance, and strength to make them winners on the court.

Stamina is another important skill. It is what keeps you going through an extra-innings ball game or a long bike ride — it means learning to keep your heart rate up for a long time. One practice for stamina is to do a "beep test" where you run back and forth on a tennis court in time to beeps that get faster and faster! A tennis player needs stamina to stay out on the court for a match that could last up to four hours.

Tennis wasn't always so tough. Fifty years ago, tennis players were not doing off-court training. They used their good serves or strokes to get them through a match. "Today you can't get away with just having the basic skills," Petras says. She says strength, speed, and power are important for today's pros — and they have to train for that.

WHAT A RELIEF!

Breaking an arm or leg is bad enough, but wearing a cast can drive you crazy. It's okay for a little while. It's nice and clean and all your friends can sign it. But after a few weeks, the skin under the cast starts to itch ... and then it starts to smell. What's a cast-wearer to do?

Leni Faas and Bill Spaeth took the problem to a chemist. He told them that the itch and smell are caused by bacteria that grow under the cast. The bacteria grow well in the warm, moist spaces between the cast and the skin.

This boy has perfected his balance and he's ready to move in any direction to hit the ball.

But you don't have to go to tennis camp or even be a tennis player to improve your flexibility, strength, speed, or stamina. Test yourself by seeing how far you can throw a baseball, how many lengths of a pool you can swim, or how many times you can jog around your block. Keep practicing at everything you do, and soon your body will be in super condition for any sport!

So, the two inventors came up with some temporary relief: "Castblast." It's a mixture of alcohol and talcum powder that can be sprayed inside the cast through a tube.

The alcohol cleans the skin and the talcum powder soaks up the moisture. But mostly, Castblast makes the skin feel better. "It feels icy cold and it lets you sleep through the night," says Faas.

— Elizabeth Keyishian

NEW FOR KNEES

Have you ever seen an athlete hurt a knee while playing sports? Well, the athlete may have torn the soft, rubbery substance, or cartilage, that protects the ends of your bones. Probably the athlete had to have X rays or even surgery so the doctor could find the problem.

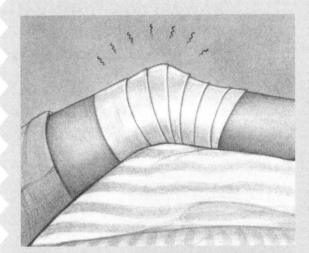

Wouldn't it be easier if the doctor just had to listen to the knee to find the problem? Now, with something called the Knee Screener created by a team of doctors at Queen's University in Belfast, Ireland, that's becoming possible. The doctor attaches three sensors to the knee. The sensors pick up the vibrations in your knee as it moves. Doctors link these vibrations to the position the knee is in and find the tear.

The technique is still experimental, but researchers hope the Knee Screener will be part of every professional sports dressing room some day!

ANiMAL

BY CAROL GOLD AND HUGH WESTRUP

Imagine trying to arm wrestle an octopus!
You'd need three friends to help you. Or how
about boxing with a kangaroo? You'd want to
make sure you were just shadowboxing because
kangaroos fight with their powerful hind legs.
With one kick, the kangaroo would have the
boxing match in the pouch ... er, bag.

**Who would be the winners
if humans really did compete in
sporting events with animals?**

Weight lifting

One day at the Bronx Zoo in New York City, a 45-kg chimpanzee lifted a weight of six times its own weight. (Champion Olympic weight lifters can lift only four times their own weight.) And how about the ant? Laboratory measurements show that an ant can pick up and carry back to its nest a rock 50 times its own weight. That would be like you toting a two-tonne elephant.

But even the mighty ant is a weakling next to the Goliath beetle — it can lift at least 850 times its own weight. If you had that much might, you could carry four school buses on your back. Goliath beetles, which live in tropical climates, are so strong that children hitch them up to toy wagons and hold beetle harness races.

ATHLETES

Long jump When it comes to the long jump, we don't do all that badly alongside the other large mammals. Humans can jump nearly nine metres, and only a few mammals can beat that — horses can jump 11 m, mountain lions 12 m, and kangaroos nearly 13 m. But the small animals jump farthest in relation to their body size. While an Olympic competitor can jump about five or six times the length of his or her own body, a jack-rabbit running to save its life can jump 11 times the length of its body. The tiny jumping mouse, which can fit into your hand, can leap more than 30 times the length of its body.

But by far the best long jumper is the flea. With legs that measure only about a tenth of a centimetre long, a flea can jump 200 times the length of its body. To beat that, a human long jumper would have to leap across five city blocks.

CHECK IT OUT! Orangutans get the measles and dogs sneeze! How are the bodies of animals like the human body? The next time you watch a TV show about animals, listen carefully for similarities between you and the exotic animals on the screen. Come to think of it — how are you and your dog or cat alike?

Swimming

When it comes to swimming, people are like fish out of water. The fastest Olympic swimmer trolls along at a mere eight kilometres per hour. A walrus can get up to about 24 km/h in water, while a leatherback turtle will hit speeds of 35 km/h.

The best swimmer among the birds is the penguin (35 km/h) and among the mammals, the dolphin (46 km/h).

But the fastest of them all is the sailfish which lives in great numbers around south Florida and the Galapagos Islands.

The sailfish has a large dorsal fin which it raises and lowers like a real sail. Sailfish have been clocked at a top speed of 110 km/h, almost twice the speed of the world's fastest nuclear submarines!

CHECK IT OUT!

Look in the library for biographies of
- Babe Didrikson
- Jackie Robinson
- Muhammed Ali

and other famous sports figures.

Running The only way a human could win this event would be in a speeding car. And you'd have to break the speed limit to overtake the cheetah which has been clocked at a top speed of 114 km/h. Olympic runners can only make it up to 44 km/h.

Few cars could beat a cheetah in a test of acceleration. The sleek, spotted African cat goes from zero to 72 km/h in a mere two seconds. How does a cheetah move so fast? Its flexible spine bends like a spring as the animal runs. This allows the cheetah to bring its back legs well in front of its front legs on each leap. At the beginning of the next leap, its spine straightens out, giving extra thrust to its strong back legs.

Arctic Mirages

BY JAY INGRAM

You've heard of mirages in hot, sandy deserts,
but could they happen in the Arctic desert?
Scientists think so.

the
if th
ligh
hap

Elevation (m)

0.4 —

0.0 —

0.0
Horizo

You
som
som

fant
mar

We
Nor
kno
rea
Nev
we

The Vikings may have seen mirages centuries ago when they first crossed the fierce North Atlantic to North America.

One of the strange dangers faced by the Vikings was the "merman" — not the famous "mermaid." The merman was a monstrous creature, part-human, part-animal, that could sometimes be seen in the Arctic, rearing up out of the water. These mermen would stand, huge and still, unlike any living creature the sailors had ever seen.

After 800 years or so, scientists in Winnipeg, Manitoba, think they've figured out what the mermen really were — mirages! Tricks played on the eye.

Turn the page to see how these Arctic mirages work.

L ate one afternoon, I packed my headlamp, some spare batteries, my camera and flash, and a chunk of cheese, and set off uphill. When I reached the edge of the woods, the sun was already sinking. Soon, streaks and spots of cool green light began to pulse in the dark. I knew they were the courting signals of the fireflies and click beetles.

The forest was also filling up with all kinds of strange sounds. Whistles, whoops, and chirpings were coming from every direction. Without the use of my eyes, my ears seemed much more sensitive. I could hear the swooping bats above me and the whining mosquitos circling my head.

As I sat on a log in the dark, I heard rustling noises in the leaves beside me. My nose was picking up the heavy perfume of flowers and the smell of decaying leaves.

Above: Adrian Forsyth in the jungle

Right: This little mouse has big eyes to help it see in the dark.

I wanted to wait as long as possible in the dark, soaking up the sounds, the smells, the feeling of night in the jungle. Then something ran across my hand. I jumped up electrified. It was time to turn on the lights.

I felt for my headlamp and switched on the light. As soon as I looked around, I realized this had been a good move. Right beside me on the log was a large scorpion armed with a long, powerful, stinging tail. That was one

nighttime sensation I did not want to experience. The scorpion was munching on a katydid, so I left it to enjoy its breakfast without my company.

Walking along the trail with my headlamp lighting the way was like walking slowly through a long dark tunnel. The forest all around me was inky black, and all my attention was focused on the narrow circle of light just

ahead of me. My eyes were watching the ground right ahead of my feet. When I wanted to look up, I had to stop and stand still to avoid crashing into trees. Moving like this was a great way to discover small animals I might miss during the day, when sunlight exposed the whole forest all at once.

I saw slippery-looking salamanders in the leaves, waiting to capture insects. In the middle of a raspberry patch, my light surprised a tiny harvest mouse not much bigger than the raspberries it was eating. It had long whiskers around its face to detect objects, and huge dark eyes for night vision. The vegetation was crawling with long-legged tree frogs whose fingers and toes ended in broad flat suckers which clung to the leaves. Their huge bulging eyes helped them see under dim light.

217

Looking for large eyes turned out to be the easiest way to find mammals. I stood still and slowly swept my headlamp through the treetops until a pair of burning red lights shone toward me from a tree. When I walked closer, I could see the lights were porcupine eyes. They were reflecting the light of my headlamp back at me. Porcupines, like most night-active mammals, have a shiny layer on the back inner surface of their eyes that helps gather light and reflect it.

To my surprise, I saw tiny eyes shining like clusters of rubies on the forest floor. When I got down on my hands and knees I discovered they were the eyes of small spiders.

Above: A porcupine with its tell-tale red eyes

Right: An anole lizard shedding its skin

Not all the animals I saw were awake. I noticed many sleeping lizards on the ferns and palm fronds beside the trail. They didn't seem to mind my light at all. The curious thing about the lizards was that they were always out on the very tips of the long dangling fronds. I wondered if the lizards were placing themselves at the very tips of the leaves as a kind of early warning system to detect approaching snakes, possums, and other animals that eat lizards. When the predator approaches, it bumps into the delicate frond. The bump alerts the lizard. I tried out my theory by gently jiggling a fern where a lizard was sleeping. It worked! The lizard let go and scuttled off as soon as it hit the ground.

I was starting to relax a little as I got used to the nightlife. But as I passed under a steep bank, my calm was interrupted by a sudden crunching, tearing sound. I stopped in my tracks and looked up. A furry brown animal

with a long dangling tail was biting into the stem of a tree fern. It was a kinkajoo ripping out the soft insides of the stem and swallowing large mouthfuls.

The kinkajoo turned toward me and was blinded by my headlamp for a minute. It couldn't see me but it could smell me, and the

218

smell was making it nervous. It hopped toward me and perched on a vine. Snuffing and snorting, it leaned down so close that I could almost touch its furry head. I knew this would be a mistake. I could see its strong claws and powerful jaws, and it looked like an animal who would defend itself. So I quickly snapped off my light.

The kinkajoo leaped by and went crashing away through the undergrowth.

I checked my watch and was startled to see that it was only eight o'clock. There was plenty of night left to enjoy. But I decided to enjoy it in a quieter, more familiar place — my home and my bed.

219

ECLIPSE

BY GREG WALZ-CHOJNACKI

Every so often, a shadow spreads
across the land. The sky darkens,
and animals become uneasy or
confused. Over parts of the Earth,
day turns to night, and the stars
come out at high noon.
It's an eclipse!
It's one of the strangest and most
interesting events the sky has to
offer. The moon passes in front
of the sun,
casting its shadow onto parts of
the Earth and the sea. Watch local
newspapers and magazines to find
out when an eclipse might be
coming your way!

you will get a chance to see something rare and exciting: the partial eclipse of the sun. But a total eclipse is even more spectacular. People travel hundreds of kilometres to watch a total eclipse— those precious minutes when the moon completely covers the sun.

During a total eclipse, scientists can learn a lot about the sun by studying its faint outer atmosphere, or the corona (cah-ROW-nah). But you don't have to be a scientist to enjoy the beauty of this delicate, pinkish veil.

During a total eclipse, the world is cast into an eerie darkness. Much of the natural world is confused by the change. Birds return to their nests to

The first reappearance of the sun at the edge of the moon produces a lovely "diamond ring."

CHECK IT OUT!

When was the last eclipse in your community? Has there ever been a total eclipse in your community? Check local records and newspapers for more information.

The last total solar eclipse was in 1991. It was such a popular event that hotel rooms in California, Mexico, and Hawaii — where the best views were — were booked two years ahead! Better book now for the next eclipse!

223

Living in the Sh

Ten years ago, I moved to Fairbanks, Alaska,
to teach, arriving just ahead of winter. I knew it would
be cold, but I didn't know it would be so dark.
In midwinter in Fairbanks, the sun stays low in the sky
and the days are short. This time-lapse photograph
shows the sun rising and setting in just three hours.
The length of the days grows shorter
and shorter until, farther north at the North Pole,
the night is exactly six months long.

BY GRANT SIMS

The ocean of night

Experiencing the night in winter in Alaska was like crossing a new frontier. Watching the stars and the northern lights was like watching a dark and mysterious ocean. I looked at the night sky with new interest and a little fear. During my second winter in Alaska, I met a scientist who had moved north because of the darkness — to study the northern lights, or *aurora borealis,* which means "dawn of the north" in Latin. These lights are caused by explosions on the sun which send electrons speeding outwards. These electrons crash into matter in the atmosphere at the top of Earth. The night sky at Fairbanks is lit by this ghostly reminder of the absent sun on about 240 nights a year.

Cheering up winter

In the Arctic, enduring the long, dark winter is made easier by the cheerfulness of the scientists who must work through the night. Biologists are delighted when they come across wakeful wolves and sleeping bears. Geophysicists, who study the Earth's crust, are awed by movements of ice over our planet's surface. At sub-zero temperatures, those who live above the Arctic Circle make the most of the short daylight hours as well as the long nights. Come summer, the day is endless. With eyes red-rimmed from tiredness, you are on the go until you drop.

For nine winters in the north, I assumed that I was going through more hours of darkness than people farther south. I thought that the North and South Poles received the most darkness on Earth. In fact, every place on Earth gets six months of light and six of darkness. Every winter, the ends of the globe get less light, but they get more light every summer. Over a year, the total of light at any point on Earth equals that at any other point.

Sun tricks

At Fairbanks, I could watch with delight the tricks the winter sun performed in the brief hours of daylight. I could see "sun dogs," or rainbows caused by ice crystals, Arctic mirages, light rings in the sky, and sometimes a green flash at dawn or dusk.

Despite these magic light shows in the sky, the long hours of winter make us panic sometimes. In autumn, as we get out our boots and down clothing to insulate us against the lightless cold, we feel like deep-sea divers plunging into a sea of night. And when the winter seems endless, we dream of those moonless summer days.

THE
SHADOW KNOWS

Ever noticed how the shadow of an object can look a lot different from the actual object? You can use that fact to turn your hands into a whole zoo full of animals.

Can you guess what "animals" the hands here are making? To make it easier, hold your hands as shown and make the shadows yourself. They'll show up best if you use a flashlight or reading lamp and cast your shadows onto a white wall.

How could you make this shadow?

Is there a difference between shadows cast by light from the sun and those cast by an electrical light? Get a friend to help you find out.

You will need:
• a comb
• a flat surface
• a sunny window
• a flashlight

Near the window, hold the comb with the tip of its teeth touching a table or other flat surface. Your friend can record how the shadows fall.

Close the curtain to block out the sunlight. Have your friend hold the flashlight about 30 cm from the comb and shine the flashlight on the comb. Record how the shadows fall.

What differences do you and your friend notice? Why do you think they happen?

— Elizabeth MacLeod

227

JAPANESE GARDENS:
In Praise of Shade

If you've ever walked into a shady garden on a hot day, you know how good it feels. The Japanese like the way it feels too — they have been using natural shade and cool, green plants in their gardens since the twelfth century.

This moss garden in Pennsylvania was created using many of the ideas of Zen gardening, including balance, privacy, and peace.

It's called Zen gardening. Zen gardens let nature take control. One of the goals of Zen gardening is to rediscover nature. Zen gardens don't have a formal plan — people teach that you use your eye and your heart to create one.